A PRAIRIE CHRISTMAS

*A Pair of Novellas Celebrating
the Age-Old Season of Love*

PAMELA GRIFFIN
MARYN LANGER

BARBOUR
PUBLISHING

Published by Barbour Publishing, Inc., P.O. Box 719, Uhrichsville, Ohio 44683, www.barbourbooks.com

Our mission is to publish and distribute inspirational products offering exceptional value and biblical encouragement to the masses.

 Member of the
Evangelical Christian
Publishers Association

Printed in the United States of America.
5 4 3 2 1

A
PRAIRIE
CHRISTMAS

ONE WINTRY NIGHT

by Pamela Griffin

Dedication

A special thank you to all the wonderful women
who helped me by critiquing this book—
Maryn L., Jill S., Paige W. D., Lena D., Anne G.,
Candice S., Erin L., Mary H., and, of course, Mom.
Also thanks to Meredith E., Pamela K. T. (O.),
and Mary C. for helping with the Nebraska
and Welsh information.

To my loving Guide, my Lord Jesus,
who's always been the Light to lead me
through the sudden storms in life.

*Charity suffereth long, and is kind; charity envieth not;
charity vaunteth not itself, is not puffed up.*
1 Corinthians 13:4

Chapter 1

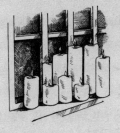

Leaning Tree, Nebraska—October 1871

H iya, Boston." With his forefinger and thumb, Craig lazily tipped the brim of his hat toward the pretty brunette.

Indignation shot through her blueberry-colored eyes. Pink stained her cheeks. Instead of answering him, Ivy Leander tossed her dark curls with a little huff and walked right past where he stood on the weathered boardwalk in front of Johnson's feed store.

Old Mr. Meyers rasped out a chuckle before she was out of hearing range. "Might as well forget that one, Craig. She's about as friendly as a pork-ee-pine with all-over body aches. And she don't seem to like you much neither."

The former cobbler from Tennessee might be right about that—for now. But Craig wouldn't let that stop him. He stared after the woman in the gray store-bought dress with the shiny ribbons. He knew the dress was store-bought because of all the gossip flying among the town's old hens ever since Gavin Morgan married Ivy's ma and brought the woman and her daughter to Leaning Tree, Nebraska, this past spring. Then, too, no store-bought dress could be found at the general store, so it must be from Boston. Under Ivy's stylish hat, out of place in this rugged town, spirals of dark curls hung, bouncing along her neck. Most women he knew wore their hair wrapped in two braids around their head or in a bun. Craig liked Ivy's way of doing her hair better.

"She sure is a feisty one," he agreed as he went back to the task of foisting the cumbersome feed sack into the rear of Mr. Meyers's wagon. He shoved the large canvas sack into place next to the farm supplies the old man had purchased.

"Thankee much, Craig." Mr. Meyers rubbed his white-whiskered jaw. "Don't know what I woulda done if you weren't here. Never woulda reckoned that young giant Tommy woulda gone and busted his leg."

"Glad to have helped," Craig said with a sincere smile. Mr. Meyers looked about as brittle as an ice-coated twig and close to being as skinny. Craig hoped the man's nephew Tommy was up to par soon.

A burst of giggling sailed across the muddy road. Craig looked to see two young women, Beth and Sally, strolling along the boardwalk. They whispered behind their hands, staring Ivy's way. Craig also turned to look. A wagon had just rumbled past where Ivy walked, spraying muddy water on the bottom of her gray dress. She stamped her kid boot, her fists pumping once at her sides, and glared at the retreating wagon.

"I hate this town!" The small growl left her throat, but it was loud enough for Craig to hear. She marched forward several more steps and turned to enter the general store. As though she sensed Craig's stare, she looked in his direction.

He dipped his head her way, tipping his hat again. She broke eye contact, slipped her hand to the top of her feathered bonnet to pat it, as if to make sure it was still in place, and marched through the door.

"Yessiree," Mr. Meyers said with a low whistle. "I sure enough do pity the poor fool who takes her for a wife."

Craig eyed the closed door of the general store a few seconds longer, then turned, the grin going wide on his face. "I reckon that'd be me, sir."

"Pardon?" Mr. Meyers pulled at his thick earlobe as if

he had wax in his ear and couldn't hear well, though the man was reputed to hear a sneeze in the next county.

"I'm the one who's going to marry Ivy Leander."

Surprise shone from Mr. Meyers's eyes, then pity. He let out a loud guffaw. "The sun must've gone to your head, boy!"

"No, sir. By this time next year, I plan to make Ivy my wife. Or my name isn't Craig Watson." He adjusted his hat, gave a jovial farewell nod, and headed toward the general store.

"Nice knowin' ya, Jim," Mr. Meyers's amused voice came from behind. "Wonder what Ivy'll think of your little plan. Care to make a wager on its success?"

Craig kept walking—not that he had any doubts concerning his claim. He just wasn't a betting man. And even if he were, Jebediah Meyers didn't usually have more than two coins to rub together after a trip to town. It would shame Craig to take money from the old man.

Ivy eyed the sparse selection of goods in the cramped store with distaste. Even the nicest ribbons and combs and whatnots for sale were a pale comparison to the quality of those found in Boston. Everything in the East was nicer, with more variety from which to choose. The stores were cleaner, too. She skirted a couple of muddy boot prints on the plank floor, scrunching her nose in disgust.

Could the fifty dollars her wealthy grandmother secretly presented to her before she left Boston even be spent in such a place? The dear woman had known how much Ivy dreaded prairie life and told her to use the money for some "little extravagance" but not to tell her mother about the gift. Yet what of that nature could be found here?

Why Mama had to go and fall in love with an un-educated farmer who chose to make his home in the prairie wilds lay beyond Ivy's scope of reasoning. Her young stepsisters certainly didn't add honey to the pot, either. Crystin and Gwen couldn't keep their hands off Ivy's things, despite Ivy's frequent complaints to her mother to have a talk with them and set them straight. Mama quietly explained to Ivy that, being so new a family, there were bound to be disturbances and issues need-ing to be ironed out, and Ivy should just be patient and let time run its course to fix things.

Ivy had been patient—up until yesterday when she found her gold-filigree garnet brooch with the seed pearls, a gift her beloved grandmother had given her, tromped into the hay-strewn ground near the pig's smelly trough. A tinge of remorse unsettled Ivy at the way she'd lit into

11

eight-year-old Crystin, and she couldn't help but remember the tears that made the child's big blue eyes glisten.

The door opened, and Craig Watson strode inside. A blacksmith by trade, he had the strong arms and hands to prove it. Tall, well-built, with his nutmeg brown eyes often dancing in amusement—no doubt at her expense—he had an annoying habit of calling her "Boston" rather than using the appropriate title of "Miss Leander," as the Bostonian gentlemen of her acquaintance had done. To their credit, a few of the male settlers in this town also addressed her properly, though most just called her "ma'am." But not Mr. Ill-mannered Blacksmith. Oh no. Not him.

"Good morning, Craig," the plump Mrs. Llewynn said from behind the counter.

"Mornin', ma'am." The timbre of his voice poured out like wild honey, smooth and warm. He caught Ivy's stare and tipped his hat, that ever-present, rakish, close-lipped grin on his tanned, all too attractive face. "Mornin'."

Ivy's heart ran a foolish little race in her bosom as it often did when he smiled her way. She snapped her focus back to the bolts of sprigged material lying on a nearby weathered table. Calico. Only poor country folk wore calico. She might as well cut holes in a feed sack and wear that.

She heard his boots clomp toward the counter at the front. Curiosity propelled her to lift her gaze a few inches. From the back, under his hat, thick clumps of wheat-colored hair brushed the bottom edge of his collar. The man was in dire need of a haircut. And a bath. Though the odors weren't exactly offensive, the smell of smoke and raw iron permeated his clothing, and fresh sweat dampened his shirt.

"What can I do for you today?" Mrs. Llewynn asked him with a wide smile, looking up from thumbing through a magazine.

"I need to get a caldron if you have one. Mine sprung a leak this morning."

"Oh, my. I sure don't, but I do have an old washtub you can use."

"I'd appreciate it." Craig tipped his hat back from his forehead. "That your latest issue of *Godey's*?"

"Yes. It just arrived yesterday."

"Excuse me?" Ivy moved forward. "Did I understand correctly? You have a recent copy of the *Godey's Lady's Book*?"

"That I do," Mrs. Llewynn said with a nod before she again looked at Craig. "I'll just go get that washtub." She left her place behind the counter and bustled to the back room. Craig nudged the corner of the magazine with two

13

fingers, pushing it at an angle. He looked down sideways, tilting his head as if to peer at the cover but not wanting to seem too interested.

Ivy stepped up beside him, almost knocking into him in her haste. "Pardon," she breathed as she slid the magazine the few inches her way for a better view. Excited, she thumbed to the first page and soon became engrossed in the illustrations, rapidly shuffling through the pages. Her hand stilled, and she sighed. "Oh, what a simply lovely gown this would make for a Christmas ball."

"I surely wouldn't mind seeing you in it," Craig's amused voice came back.

Ivy's hand froze at the top corner of the next page before she could turn it. Heat flamed her cheeks, and she snapped her gaze from the illustrations of velvet and ribbons and bustles to Craig's laughing eyes.

"Oh, my" was all she could think to say. She wasn't sure which embarrassed her more—his highly personal and improper remark or the fact that in her great excitement to find a link with civilization, she had acted like a hoyden and pushed him aside to snatch the magazine away. Miss Lucy Hadmire of the elite ladies' academy Ivy once attended would be shocked to have witnessed her prize pupil's performance.

"I do apologize," she murmured, snatching her hand

from the magazine. "I didn't mean to be rude."

His thick, neat brows lifted in wry amusement, as if reminding her of the irony of that statement, and another wave of embarrassment swept over her. Ever since she'd stepped off the wagon that first day in Leaning Tree, she'd been nothing but rude to this man. Yet such rudeness developed from the dread that he might one day become interested in her, as his looks toward her implied. She could never stoop so low as to marry a farmer, much less a blacksmith! Her husband would be an educated man of considerable means, as her doctor-father had been.

"Well, now, Boston, ladies' magazines aren't exactly of interest to me," he said with another of his irritating grins. "So look as much as you'd like."

That name again. *Insufferable man.*

She turned on her heel. "I'll come back another time." Before he could let loose with another teasing remark, she flounced out of the store.

Chapter 2

Two days after his encounter with Ivy, Craig brushed at the sweat dripping from his brow with the back of one forearm, then set the glowing yellow iron over the horn of the anvil and resumed pounding it into a horseshoe shape. Regardless of the fact that the huge doors of the smithy were rolled open as far as they would go, it was still muggy and unseasonably warm.

He whistled a tune, though the jarring strikes of the hammer ringing off metal blocked most of it. Whistling helped him relax, and he did it for that reason alone. As he worked and the sparks flew, he thought about Ivy. His mind jumped back to the first day he'd met her.

Plump and pretty, she had just stepped off a dusty wagon that rolled to a stop not far from where Craig worked. A thinner woman stepped to the parched ground behind her. She had the same blue eyes and was older by about twenty years. Then Gavin Morgan stretched his short, compact build from the wagon and helped a petite elderly woman to alight. Ivy had stood eyeing her surroundings with a mixture of frank despair and cold disdain. As Craig approached, he could almost feel the thick frost coating her, though the day was about as hot as bacon fat sizzling on a griddle.

"Afternoon, ladies." Craig had tipped his hat to the women, then shook his friend's hand. "Gavin, good to have you back." His gaze again settled on Ivy. "Welcome to Leaning Tree."

The younger woman gave what Craig thought might be considered a nod. It was so slight, he wasn't sure.

Gavin presented his new wife, Eloise, and his mother, also referring to Ivy as "Eloise's daughter," then he walked into the general store with the two older women following. Before Ivy could join them, Craig thought up something to say. "So, where are you from?"

She looked down her nose at him. "It really isn't proper for us to converse without first being *formally* introduced. But to answer your question, I'm from Boston. That's in Massachusetts, incidentally."

"Really. You don't say." He felt a grin curl up his

mouth at her high-handed approach toward what she considered his ignorance, and he pushed back his hat from his forehead, deciding to play along.

"Well, now, ma'am, 'round these here parts, the most formal interductions sound something like, '*Here, soooo-eeeeee!*'" He let the words loose in a squeal similar to the one he'd heard Mrs. Llewynn use when calling her hogs to their meal.

Ivy's blueberry eyes widened in surprise, and she took a quick step back, almost tripping over the warped boardwalk. She put her gloved hand to the nearby hitching post to steady herself.

"'Course, that approach only works when you're socializin' with the hogs," Craig continued matter-of-factly. "When you wanna talk to the chickens, you should say, 'Here, chick, chick, chick, chick, chick, chick!'" He let the phrase jump from his mouth in a rapid stream of bulletlike words, then feigned a look of innocent realization. "But I reckon what you actually was meanin' was a formal interduction with the people 'round these here parts."

"Of course I meant the people," she snapped. "Why should I wish to socialize with the pigs?"

"Hogs, ma'am. They's different than pigs, but prob'ly a whole lot more sociable than mosta the folks here in Leaning Tree." He leaned in close as though about to reveal a secret. "Smarter, too," he confided in a low voice. "Why, ole Stony Jack's hog can count to ten while most people 'round here cain't even read nor write."

She crossed her arms over her frilly, lace-covered blouse, her reticule dangling from one wrist. "Oh, really! Surely you don't expect me to believe such nonsense?"

He crossed a hand over his heart. "Sure as I'm standin' here and the day is warm. Where'd you say you was from again?"

"Boston." She frowned. "Must I write the name on my forehead for you to remember it?"

Craig held back a chuckle. "Oh no, ma'am. I think I can remember it next time around."

And he had—calling her "Boston" from that day on. It fit her, from the top of her sassy, feathered hat to the leather soles of her fancy kid boots and all points between. Still, there was something about Ivy Leander that aroused more than his curiosity. She intrigued him; he'd never met a woman like her. All spit and fire but with a noticeable softness touching her expression when she didn't know she was being watched. And Craig had done his share of watching these past months.

At the harvest dance, he'd even asked her to take a spin with him around the huge wooden platform built just for the occasion. She had snubbed his invitation with a brisk "No, thank you," looking away as if he were no more than a pesky horsefly buzzing about. Yet Craig had made up his mind that he wouldn't let that deter him from his plan to court her. He'd caught Ivy doing her share of watching him when she didn't think he was looking. She didn't fool him one bit; Ivy appeared as interested in Craig as he was in her. Underneath all that lacy froth and those fancy ribbons, he imagined he'd find a woman with a tender heart. At least he hoped so. Everyone from Mr. Meyers to the old doc thought him foolish in his persistence to try to win her affections. Maybe he was, at that.

Seeing that the metal had lost most of its color, Craig stopped his pounding and whistling and twisted around in a half-circle, intending to poke the iron back into the fire blazing yellow in the forge, to get it to the right temperature again. To his surprise, he heard the next notes of his tune faintly whistled behind him before cutting off abruptly.

He spun around in the direction from which he thought the notes were coming in the dim light of his three-walled shop. No one stood there. One hand still wrapped around the handle of his hammer, the other around the tongs, he made a slow circle of the room. In a dark corner, he noticed one of his work aprons crumpled on the floor—then saw it move. Craig thought about the recent theft of one of Gladys Llewynn's chickens.

"You come on out from there," he said, tightening his grip on the hammer. "I don't want any trouble." He took a step closer. "Come on out, I said."

A stiff rustle of cloth was followed by the sight of a small girl popping her head up, her eyes wide with uncertainty. Beads of sweat trickled down her temples, and wisps of damp hair stuck to her skin. As stifling hot as it was in the smithy, that was no surprise.

Craig relaxed. "Amy Bradford, what are you doing hiding in that corner? You come on out from there. Do your parents know you're here?"

Amy hurried to stand and shook her head, her two corn-silk-colored braids swishing against her brown calico dress. "Miss Johnson let us out early today. I'm hidin' from Wesley."

Once classes were dismissed, the brother and sister often played such games on the rare occasions they did attend school. Yet Craig wasn't sure he approved of them playing in his workplace. Before he could answer, a young boy's voice called from outside.

"Amy Lamey, I know you're in there!"

The girl's mouth compressed at the nickname her brother used. "Don't tell him where I am," she whispered, putting a finger to her lips before diving back under the apron and curling into a ball.

Craig blew out a lengthy breath and shook his head. He couldn't find it in his heart to begrudge the two a little fun. Coming from a family of fourteen kids, Amy and Wesley were the middle children, responsible for a good portion of the chores. They barely found time to play. Of course, that was the lot of most prairie children.

"I heard you talkin', so's I know you're in here." Nine-year-old Wesley, with his carrot top of curly hair, moved into the smithy as if he owned the place. "Howdy, Mr. Watson."

Craig nodded in greeting. Accustomed to customers milling about the place while they waited on orders to be filled, he heated the horseshoe again, forged a turned-up clip at the front to protect the horse's hoof, then bored eight holes into it with his pritchel tool to hold the nails. After rounding the ends, he doused it in Mrs. Llewynn's nearby washtub filled almost to the brim with cool water. A loud *hisssss* escaped, and steam sprayed his face. With the iron now cooled so that he could handle it without burning himself, he hung it over the anvil's horn to join the other three horseshoes there.

"Guess who I saw mailin' a letter today?" the boy asked, reminding Craig of his presence.

"You still here?"

"Aw, come on, Mr. Watson. Guess."

"I wouldn't have the vaguest idea." Craig wiped the sweat and grime from his hands down the front of his leather apron. At present, the schoolhouse shared its space with the postal office—Mr. Owen taking over one corner of the building to conduct his business there.

"Miss Uppity from Boston," the boy announced.

Craig bit back the grin that wanted to jump to his mouth at the boy's nickname for Ivy. He hung his tools on their spot near the bellows. "You shouldn't call her that, Wesley. It's not nice to call people names."

"That's what Ma calls her when she's talking about her to Pa." The boy headed to a hitching post several feet away, where a skittish horse waited to be shod, and hoisted himself up to sit on the wood. The bay whinnied a greeting, and Wesley looped a chubby arm around its neck in a brief hug. " 'Sides, she is uppity. She comes to town 'most every week to look through those fancy ladies' magazines of Mrs. Llewynn's, but she doesn't talk to hardly no one."

"Maybe she doesn't know what to say. You ever talk to her?"

Wesley scrunched up his mouth in a guilty expression. "Naw, but Amy tried today durin' lunch. Miss Ivy got all funny lookin', like she didn't want nobody knowin' her business. She was mailin' a letter but kept lookin' behind her, like she was afraid someone would see. Amy walked up to her and asked her who the letter was for, but she didn't pay Amy no mind."

Craig tucked the words away to ponder later. He donned his hat, picked up his toolbox, and walked out in the sunshine toward the boy. "There's no law that says she has to tell two bean sprouts her business."

Wesley chuckled and began swinging his short legs, as if daring gravity to keep him upright. Craig wondered how come the boy didn't fall, balanced as he was on such a narrow beam.

"Is it true what Mr. Meyers said?" the boy asked. "That you told him you're gonna marry up with Miss Ivy someday?"

Surprised, Craig set his tools down with a bang. "Where'd you hear that?"

"Just around."

Craig grimaced. He never should have told Mr. Meyers his plans. The last thing he needed was for Ivy to hear such news through the town's busybodies. "Know why God gave you two ears and one mouth?"

Wesley shook his head.

"So you'd spend more time listening to the teachings

of your elders and less time talking about matters that aren't any of your business." Craig released a long breath. "As long as you're here, put yourself to use. That horse seems to like you, but I've been having trouble with it all morning. When I took the old shoes off, she almost bit me. I need you to hold the halter and talk nice and easy to her while I shoe her."

Wesley's face brightened as he slid off the hitching post. "Does this mean I can be your apprentice?"

Craig's eyebrows lifted. "Where'd you learn such a big word?"

"At school. We was studyin' on colonial times when they had them apprentices. Some of us even had to learn us a poem about a village blacksmith. I'd like to be a blacksmith someday. I learn real fast. So can I be your apprentice?" he asked again.

"Don't know about that. You're a mite small yet." At the boy's downcast eyes, Craig relented. "Give yourself a few more years to fill out, and I'll consider it. That is, if your ma and pa agree. Now hold the horse steady. While I'm pounding these nails in, I don't want her suddenly getting skittish so that I end up missing the horseshoe and hitting my leg instead."

The boy was as good as his word and held the horse while Craig drove the short nails into the holes of the shoes, fastening them to the horse's hooves. The studs on the bottom would give the horse traction over icy roads once the snows hit. Craig had already fitted his own horse with similar shoes and was surprised the town hadn't received any freezing weather yet.

"All done." He removed the hind hoof of the horse from his lap, straightened from his bent position, and turned to face the bay and the boy who held her. "You get on home now, Wesley. Your ma will be worried."

Wesley scratched the back of his curly head. "She does worry an awful lot, don't she? Pa says she's fractious 'cuzza the twins. Bye, Mr. Watson."

Before the boy walked more than five steps, Craig called out. "Wait! Aren't you forgetting something?"

Wesley turned and lifted his shoulders in a shrug. "Uh, don't think so."

Craig raised his eyebrows. "Your little sister?"

"Oh, Amy," he said as if just remembering her name. "I forgot about her."

"That's what I figured," Craig muttered, heading into the smithy. He wondered why Amy hadn't made her presence known before this. Wesley had been at the smithy for the better part of an hour. When he hunkered down in the corner where he'd found her, Craig had his answer. The girl lay fast asleep under the leather apron.

For a moment, he studied her rosy cheeks and the tendrils of light-colored hair sticking to her face. Her expression was peaceful, like an angel's. He hoped to have a little girl like Amy someday—several of them. And a passel of boys, too. He wondered if Ivy liked kids.

Craig put his hand to the girl's bony shoulder and gently shook it. "Amy? It's time to wake up and go home now. The smithy's no place for little sprouts like you."

She blinked her eyes open, then sat up and rubbed them. "Oh, hi, Mr. Watson," she said sleepily. "Is it mornin'?"

"I hope not. Actually, you've been here for almost an hour, since the schoolmarm dismissed you from school anyway."

"Oh!" The girl threw off the apron and scrambled to a stand. "I have to get home and help Ma with the ironin' and cookin'. Bye, Mr. Watson!" She raced out of the smithy, soon catching up with her brother, who was waiting for her on the road. Ivy came into view, walking in their direction. She looked at the children, then darted a glance toward the smithy.

Craig smiled and tipped his hat her way.

Hurriedly she refocused on the road. Skirts a-swaying, she increased her pace and hotfooted it in the direction of her stepfather's soddy. Bottling his irritation at the latest snub, Craig watched her a while longer, shook his head, then turned back to finish his long list of tools needing forged or mended.

Morning sunshine appeared to illuminate the white-painted, timbered house at the far end of town. Ivy turned wistful eyes upon the two-story structure as she walked past. Modest in size, it was still a lot nicer than any of the other six buildings that made up Leaning Tree. And certainly a great deal more refined than the house of sod belonging to her mother's new husband. Still, it was nowhere near comparable to her grandmother's stately home in Boston, looming at the end of a tree-lined street.

Ivy halted her steps and further studied the building before her. Lace curtains at the windows. A stone chimney at the side. At least the white timbered house belonging to the Pettigrasses was respectable. People were meant to live in sturdy buildings with wooden floors and pretty rugs. Not underneath earth and grass like bugs and animals.

A petite, brown-haired woman stepped onto the porch and began to shake out a blanket in the direction the wind was blowing. Catching sight of Ivy, she smiled.

"Hulloa, Ivy! You come to town often, indeed,"

Winifred Pettigrass called in the lilting Welsh accent that all the Morgans and a few other families in town shared.

"Yes," Ivy called back. With nothing better to do after the morning chores her mother assigned her, she often preferred to spend time thumbing through the pages of the ladies' magazines and perusing the items at the general store, though she still hadn't found anything appropriate to buy. Since her stepfather's homestead was close to town, the walk was short, less than two miles.

"Can you come inside and sit with us for tea?" Winifred called out.

Ivy would like nothing better than to sit in a real chair and drink from a fine china cup, but she shook her head. "I can't. I promised Mother I'd be home to help her with the noon meal."

"Another time, then, while the weather is nice. Go you and tell that dada of yours he must come, too. Never will I understand that man and how his mind thinks."

Her words were cheery. Ivy had been in Leaning Tree long enough to realize what the woman's mood meant. Winifred Pettigrass wanted something from her brother, Ivy's stepfather. How different the two siblings were! Winifred had married a wealthy man who worked for the railroad and originally had come to town as a surveyor, where he'd met Winifred. The spry woman appreciated

the finer things in life, as did Ivy, while Ivy's new stepfather was content to live like a mole and toil the earth to
produce wheat and corn.

Winifred's mother came through the open door.
"Good day to you, Ivy," she said. "You be certain and tell
that son of mine I said to come. Three weeks now, I see
nothing of him."

"I'll tell him," Ivy called back and continued down
the road. Gavin's mother was the initial reason her stepfather had gone to Boston this past spring. Weak from
the voyage to America years ago, Bronwyn Morgan
stayed with a relative while Gavin settled his claim and
built his home in Nebraska.

How unfortunate for Ivy that Gavin chose this past
year to collect his mother—and that Ivy's mother had
been the one strolling down the sidewalk when Gavin
approached asking for directions. Two weeks later they
married—scandalous to Ivy and her grandmother's way
of thinking, but necessary since Gavin had to return to
his homestead and needed a wife and a mother for his
two daughters. Eloise Leander had been only too happy
to comply, dragging along her only daughter with her.

When Ivy begged to remain in Boston with her
grandmother, her mother flatly refused, stressing they
were a family and would remain one. And so, one minute

Ivy was dancing at a ball with the cream of Boston society. The next she was whisked away and picking up cow patties for fuel with the same gloves she'd worn to the ball.

Ivy sighed at the memory of those chaotic first few months in learning a new way of life. She focused on the road before her. A sea of undulating grass higher than her head flanked both sides of the muddy lane. Skirting the holes filled with rainwater, Ivy was glad she'd given in to common sense last week and had bought the clunky but serviceable footwear at the general store. Her soft kid boots never would have withstood this! At least, underneath her long skirts, the ugly new shoes couldn't be seen.

Hearing a child softly crying, Ivy lifted her gaze off the puddles and spotted Amy Bradford kneeling at the edge of the road. A bunch of cracked eggs littered the ground in front of the fair-haired girl. Yellow yolks mixed with the clear pool of liquid, which seeped near Amy's threadbare dress.

"Oh, Ma's gonna be so mad at me!" The nine-year-old lifted pale green eyes to Ivy and wiped the backs of her fingers over wet cheeks. "I walked all the way from home and was so careful. But this puddle was deeper than I thought, and I twisted my foot."

Ivy decided not to ask why the child would deliberately step into a puddle. "Are you hurt?" She bent down, careful not to ruin her dress.

"No, but the eggs are. What am I gonna tell Ma? She's already mad at me for stayin' so long at the smithy's two days ago and comin' home late. She needed to stay with the twins—they's awful fractious with the teething—and she told me to take the eggs to Mrs. Llewynn this morning. Ma wants to get Clarence a warm coat before the snows come. And Wesley needs shoes. They ain't got none that'll fit, and Ma's been takin' eggs every morning so's she can save enough money to buy some."

Ivy knew that, with fourteen children to raise, the Bradfords barely had enough to get by. Their sod house was even smaller than the one Ivy was forced to live in with her mother, stepfather, and two stepsisters, and Amy's home contained only one window with a cracked pane.

"How many eggs did you have with you?" Ivy asked.

"Fifteen. One's okay, though." Amy reached in the basket beside her and held up a brown oval that had somehow missed destruction.

Ivy held out her hand for the lone egg and inspected the shell. It bore a faint, hairline crack. She reached inside her reticule and withdrew a coin. "There you are."

Amy stared at the shiny dime in Ivy's hand as though puzzled. "What's that for?"

"Your egg. I'm buying it."

"But"—Amy's light brows sailed up—"that's more'n Mrs. Llewynn pays for the whole basket!"

"That's all right. I'm fond of eggs."

"A whole dime for one egg?" Amy sounded as if she still couldn't believe it.

Ivy shrugged. "If you'd rather not sell it. . ."

"Oh no." Amy grabbed the dime with dirt-stained fingers. "I wouldn't want ta de-prive you of your egg, Miss Leander." She used a version of the saying Ivy had often heard Mr. Bradford use.

Ivy carefully set the egg at the bottom of her reticule. "Good. Then it appears we've struck a bargain."

The child seemed to consider before a sly smile lifted the corners of her mouth. "Anytime you want more, you let me know, and I'll be sure and save you some."

Ivy laughed, the sound trilling through the air. "I'll do that, Amy." The grin was still on her face as she watched the girl gather her empty basket and head for home. Suddenly Ivy noticed a wagon coming her way. As the rider neared, her heart plummeted, then lifted, almost soaring above the clouds like an eagle. She pressed her hand to her bosom in a futile effort to quell the rapid beating and averted her gaze past the wagon.

"Mornin', Boston," Craig said, pulling his horse to a stop beside her.

Despite her desire not to pay him any heed, she darted a glance his way. He tipped his battered brown hat, giving her that lazy smile.

She offered a brief nod in an effort to be polite.

"Can I give you a ride home?"

"We're going in opposite directions."

"It won't be any trouble for me to turn my horse around. And your father's claim is close to town."

"Stepfather, you mean. He's not my real father."

Craig didn't reply. Feeling flustered and wishing she hadn't blurted out what she had, Ivy looked back down the road. "Thanks for the offer, but I'd rather walk."

"You sure?" His voice was gentle.

"Yes. As you pointed out, it's not far, and I enjoy the exercise."

"Okay. If you're sure." His warm brown eyes never left her face, and she felt the blush rise to her cheeks. His look reminded her that she was an unmarried woman and he was an unmarried man. A rather attractive unmarried man, even with that slight bend in his nose and his untamed hair, which grew a little long over the ears.

"I—I have to go now," she said quickly, moving away as she spoke. She set off at a walking-run for the first several feet, then slowed to a more moderate pace. However, her heart didn't slow one bit.

What was she thinking? She could never be interested in anyone from this godforsaken little town tucked away in the middle of nowhere! Even if the man wasn't a farmer and did hold what her mother had informed Ivy was one of the most respected trades in the township, Craig Watson still lived like a pauper in one cramped room adjoining his shop. He didn't even own a decent home—not that she could think of the soddies that most people from these parts lived in as decent. Yet they *were* houses with windows and doors.

With each step she took, Ivy's resolve strengthened. She would keep as far away as she could from the town blacksmith.

Chapter 3

The wind howled outside the soddy as Ivy concentrated on helping her mother hang the wash over the clothesline extending from one end of the dirt-brick wall to the other. Cold weather had hit with a vengeance, and this week's washing needed to be done inside the crowded front room. The family's faithful guard dog, Old Rufus, snoozed at his usual place near the cookstove, and Ivy had to step over the old hound more than once as she went about her task.

" *'Under a spreading chestnut tree, the village smithy stands,'* " Gwen suddenly quoted as she scrubbed a shirt on the washboard. " *'The smith, a mighty man is he, with large and sinewy hands; and the muscles of his brawny arms are strong as iron bands...'* "

"Must you recite that now?" Ivy asked her stepsister,

perturbed when an image of Craig Watson breezed past the shuttered door of her mind. It had been difficult to bar invasive thoughts of the man ever since she'd last seen him, when he offered her a ride home in his wagon. Now the poem brought vivid pictures to mind.

The eleven-year-old turned solemn blue eyes Ivy's way. "I'm supposed to know Henry Wadsworth Longfellow's poem by tomorrow, when Mr. Rayborne will make me stand up in front of class to recite it. I have to practice." She began scrubbing again. "*His hair is crisp, and black, and long, his face is like the tan; His brow is wet with honest sweat, He earns whate'er he can. . .'*"

"I'm going outside to get some air," Ivy muttered, grabbing her woolen cloak.

Her mother's gentle gaze met hers from across the room, where she stirred lye-water in a kettle heating over the fire. "While you're out, please gather more fuel, Ivy."

"Yes, Mama." Ivy grimaced in distaste but wrapped a scarf around her head, pulled on her discolored ball gloves, and reached for a nearby basket. She despised this chore above all others, but the fire was getting low, and she was the only one available to do it.

A bitter, cold wind chapped her face and bit into her, almost sweeping her the rest of the way outside. She struggled with the door to close it. Searching the frozen ground for the brown lumps, she walked a short distance until she found some. Scarcity of trees in the area made this type of fuel a necessity. Wrinkling her nose in distaste, she picked up the hardened cow patty with gloved fingers and quickly dropped it into the basket. She'd kept her old ball gloves for just this purpose. She wouldn't dream of touching the disgusting things with her bare hands as her stepsisters did!

Soon her basket was filled, and Ivy straightened. Her lower back had cramped from bending over so much, but she wasn't about to rub the ache out with the glove she'd just used. As she trudged against the wind and back to the sod house built of "Nebraska marble," as the locals were fond of calling the earthen bricks, she critically appraised it. Even prettying the name didn't change its appearance, making Ivy certain that the man who had coined the phrase did so out of a warped sense of humor. Their home was dirt with dead, brown grass growing on its roof. And the fuel for their fire was dried cow manure. If her grandmother could see the depths to which her only granddaughter had fallen, she would likely have a fit of apoplexy.

"Well, I think she's horrid!" Gwen's voice coming from around the other side of the soddy brought Ivy up short. She hesitated at the rear of her stepfather's home, wondering if she should make her presence known or keep quiet.

"I hate her," Gwen added, her words emphatic. "She thinks she owns the world and everyone's supposed to wait on her."

"She does do her part of the chores," Crystin reminded. "And Dada says it's not right to hate."

"Maybe. But just by looking at her face, you can tell that she clearly thinks all work is beneath her. And she doesn't do half of what she should. Miss Ivy, queen of Boston society." Her voice took on an affected tone. "You, girl, iron my gloves and darn my stockings. *I'm* going to the ball!"

Crystin giggled. "You can't iron gloves, Gwen."

"I know. But if she had her way, she'd probably give the order to have it done. She's so mean and bossy. The way she yelled at you when her stupid old brooch went missing is proof."

"But I did take it to look at it." Crystin sounded both repentant and puzzled.

"Yes, but she has so many fancy things. She could share instead of flaunting them in our faces like she's better than us. Not everyone has a mother or grandmother who has pretty things to give."

"You mean us?" Crystin's voice was solemn. "Was our

mama poor when our dada met her?"

"She had the riches that counted. Inside beauty is what Dada called it. Sweetness of spirit."

"Do you remember her?"

"Some. Not a lot."

"Me, either." There was a short pause. "Gwen, do you like our new mama, even if she is from Boston where the rich people live?"

"She's a lot nicer than Ivy. Yeah, I like her."

It was a moment before Crystin spoke again. "Is our dada poor?"

"No, leastways not poor like we were in Wales when we lived in the mining camp. But you were too young to remember those days. Now then, cheer up, Crystin. Who needs Miss Uppity's old Boston things anyway?"

The girls' voices grew stronger, and Ivy ducked around the opposite corner before they came into view. From her hiding place, she saw that between them they held a large pail and were headed in the direction of a nearby stream. Probably to get more rinse water.

"I think she's sad," Crystin said. "Because she don't fit in. That's what Maryanne says."

"She could fit in if she wanted to," Gwen shot back. "She just doesn't want to."

Although the words were accurate, they cut Ivy to the

quick. She never entertained any doubts that her new stepsisters held anything but dislike for her, though the little one seemed to like her a bit. She'd taken up for her, anyway. Yet why should Ivy care?

She stiffened her back and walked to the front of the soddy, against the wind, letting it dry the few unexplainable tears that teased the corners of her eyes. The girls were right. She did not belong. So maybe it was time to go back to where she did.

Craig worked the lever of the huge bellows, fanning air over the fire to get it hot enough to repair a plow. His mind went to thoughts of Ivy. Weeks ago when he'd seen her on the road, after delivering an order to an old farmer who didn't get around as well as he used to, Craig had been touched to watch the encounter between her and Amy. It didn't take a lot of figuring to realize what must have happened. Craig had perfect vision and hadn't been so far away that he couldn't spot the cracked eggs and overturned basket at the side of the road. He had watched Ivy take an egg from Amy's outstretched hand, then give her something in return.

The girl's jubilant face afterward as she turned in his direction and ran for home—like a shining sunbeam parting the gray sky—made it obvious that Ivy had paid a handsome price for the hen offering. Ivy *did* have a good heart underneath all those ribbons and furbelows. He'd known it all along. And hearing her laughter caress the chill air, Craig's own heart had soared within his chest. Her laugh reminded him of small tinkling bells and produced a smile on his face, a smile that stretched his lips even now.

Seeing by the white color of the fire that he'd made it too hot, Craig stopped fanning the flames and grabbed his washer. He immersed the bundle of tied-together twigs in water, then flicked the drops over the blaze to bring it down to a steady yellow glow. Thinking about Ivy was breaking his concentration, and that could prove dangerous. Besides, he had another busy day ahead.

Craig had finished up five of his orders when young Wesley ran into the smithy. "Mr. Owen said to tell you something came for you today by freight wagon," he blurted, out of breath. "I have to get home now, or Pa'll tan my hide."

Before Craig could respond, Wesley was gone. Craig eyed the sawhorse table along one wall, holding the orders still needing to be filled, then looked at what he'd accomplished that afternoon. Deciding it wouldn't hurt to take a short break, he put his tools away, exchanged his leather apron for his coat, and settled his hat firmly on his head.

Once outside, he moved against the cold wind toward the opposite edge of town that held the school and post office. The sky was blue and clear, and the sun gleamed off the windows of the modest-sized building. Inside and to the right, a colorful blanket hung from the ceiling. Through the gap, empty benches revealed that school was out, though the young teacher still sat behind her desk. To Craig's left, a customer stood in front of Mr. Owen's counter, and Craig's stomach did a little rollover when he saw who it was.

"Miss Leander," Mr. Owen patiently stated, "you should cut some words from that telegram to make it shorter. I charge by the word, you know."

"Yes, I know. However, every word is essential to the message."

"I understand that, ma'am, but, well, for example, this part: 'It is imperative that I hear from you before the snows begin to fall and travel becomes difficult. I am most eager to return to Boston within the next two weeks.' Well, now, ma'am. That's repeating something you said in the first sentence."

Craig's heart dropped to his boot tips. Ivy was leaving?

He shuffled his foot, unintentionally gaining her attention. She looked over her shoulder. Her eyes widened when she saw him, and her face paled.

"Hello, Boston," Craig said quietly.

"How much of that did you hear?" Her blue eyes were anxious.

"Enough to know that you plan on breaking your poor ma's heart."

Her mouth thinning, Ivy faced Mr. Owen. "I want the entire message telegraphed. I can pay for it."

The bearded man shook his head but didn't pursue his arguments. "There's a package over there for you, Craig. For some reason, it got dropped off here instead of at Mrs. Llewynn's."

Craig nodded his thanks and went to retrieve what he saw was a crate. His new caldron must have arrived. Seeing it was too big to carry, he decided to come back for it with a wagon later. He'd already settled all accounts with Mrs. Llewynn, so the caldron was his. After giving a solemn nod to Mr. Owen along with a brief explanation that he'd be back soon, then a nod to Ivy, who hesitantly turned to glance at him, Craig exited the building.

Ivy concluded her business with the postal clerk. Taking a deep breath, she stepped outside. She'd half-expected Craig to be waiting for her, so she wasn't at all surprised to see him leaning against a hitching post, his arms crossed. What did surprise her was his somber appearance, so much different from the usual one with the expression lines ready to stretch out in amusement.

She moved down the road, intending to ignore him.

"Why are you leaving us, Boston?" He straightened as she walked past, his long legs easily matching her stride.

"I don't see that it's any of your business."

"Maybe not. But you're going to hurt a lot of people by your decision to go."

"I don't belong here. This isn't my home and never has been."

"Do you really think you've given it a decent enough try?"

Needled by his words, she stopped walking and spun to face him. "Just what difference does it make to you, Mr. Watson? I should think you'd be glad to see me go. I haven't exactly been sociable toward you—toward anyone here."

A boyish grin lifted the corners of his mouth. "Not even to the hogs or the chickens?"

She felt her own lips lift upward in a smile, surprising her. She wanted to remain annoyed with this man but found it difficult to do so. "No, definitely not to them. Incidentally, I discovered you were right about Mr. Stony Jack's hog being able to 'count.' Although my stepfather explained away the incident as Mr. Stone teaching his animal to fetch objects rather than the hog itself being intelligent. Still, I suppose I do owe you an apology for that first day we met. I was upset and weary from the train ride, and I, um, acted rather supercilious toward you."

"Oh, now I wouldn't have gone and called you conceited, exactly. More sure of yourself and everybody else than anything." His grin widened.

The man was a scholar? Amazing. Ivy hadn't reckoned on him having enough schooling to possess any knowledge of the word she'd used to describe her bad behavior. "Then I'm forgiven?"

"I don't hold grudges."

"Thank you." She hesitated. "About what happened in there just now—I would appreciate it if you'd keep this our little secret. I don't wish for anyone to know of my plans."

"You planning on running away in the middle of the night?"

"Of course not! I simply want to approach my mother with the news when I feel the timing is appropriate."

He studied her a long moment. Uneasy, she glanced away from the steady look in his eyes. "I'll keep your secret," he finally said, "but on one condition."

A sense of misgiving made her gather her brows. "What condition?"

"That you let me take you to the church meeting next Sunday and go on an outing with me afterward."

"Church meeting?"

"You hadn't heard? A preacher is coming through here next week. We'll meet in the schoolhouse for services."

"No, I hadn't heard." Ivy thought quickly. A few hours with the man seemed a small price to pay for his silence. "All right, I'll go with you."

The warmth of his smile took her breath away. "I'll be looking forward to it, Boston. Well, I should get back to work now. I have orders to fill. Afternoon." With a quirky tip of his dusty hat in farewell, he headed down the road to his smithy.

Ivy continued to stare after Craig until he reached the huge doors of the building, then she realized what she was doing. With a frown, she shook herself out of her trance and walked in the direction of her stepfather's claim.

Chapter 4

I doubt he'll come. The snow is too much like ice for a wagon."

At Crystin's solemn words to Ivy, she looked out the window again, all hopes fading. The light from the morning's gray skies revealed a world clothed in a blanket of white stretching as far as the eye could see. Crystin was right. It was doubtful Craig would show. Ivy smoothed the skirt of one of her best dresses, a rich maroon brocade embellished with black ribbons matching the one she'd woven into her hair. Around her neck she wore her garnet brooch on another black velvet ribbon, and her fingers went to the stone, tracing its square outline. She told herself that she was relieved Craig hadn't shown, that this released her from their agreement. Yet the feelings coursing through her were not those of gladness.

"Never mind, Ivy." Her mother's soft voice broke through her thoughts. "We have each other, and we can read from the Holy Bible as we always do."

Ivy glanced at her mother, and concern replaced disappointment. She didn't look at all well. Her face was drawn, and her eyes had lost the luster that usually made them shimmer like precious sapphires.

Ivy went to kneel beside her chair and took her hand. "Mama, aren't you feeling well?"

"Of course, I'm fine. Just a little stomach upset. Hand me my Bible, dearest."

Ivy did so, and her mother opened the gilt-edged book she'd brought with her from Boston, reverently touching the pages as she skimmed through them. Her stepfather couldn't read English, though he spoke it, but he also often spoke in Welsh to his girls to keep their language from dying. Still, Ivy noticed that he seemed to derive great satisfaction from listening to Mama read the English words in her soothing voice.

" 'Behold, how good and how pleasant it is when brethren dwell together in unity. . . .' " As her mother continued to read the passage from Psalms, Ivy inwardly squirmed, though outside she remained as still as she'd been taught. Afterward, her mother closed the book, and no one spoke for a moment.

"Dada, when will Uncle Dai come to see us?" Gwen asked.

The question surprised everyone and seemed to hang in the air. Ivy knew the girls had been taught not to speak unless they were spoken to. She glanced at her stepfather to gauge his reaction. His face grew red, and he looked away toward the cookstove. "He chose the road to take. No one forced it upon him."

"But can he not just come see us?" Gwen insisted softly. "Nana says the same thing Mama does—family is important. Won't you write a letter to Uncle Dai and ask him to come, like Nana wants? He can stay with Aunt Winifred, since they're making their home into a boardinghouse."

"Gwendolyn! That is enough. I will have no more talk on the matter."

Ivy jumped. Even Old Rufus lifted his head off his paws to look at his master. Ivy had never before heard her stepfather raise his tone in anger, and she studied him curiously. Just what kind of man was this Uncle Dai to get such a rise from Gavin?

"I'm sorry, Dada." Gwen's lower lip trembled, and her eyes grew moist. Gavin held out his hand to his daughter, and she went to hug him.

Before Ivy could dwell more deeply on the subject of

Uncle Dai, the sound of faint bells came from outside, growing louder. Old Rufus pricked his ears and padded to the door, fully alert, his tail wagging. He let out a bark. Crystin darted to the window.

"It's Mr. Watson!" she cried. "And he's in a sleigh!"

Ivy quickly rose to see, Gwen right behind her. Sure enough, Craig sat inside a sleigh being pulled by his dark gray horse. Bells rang from the harness, and Ivy wondered if Craig had made them.

Crystin turned excitedly. "Can we go, Mama? Can we?"

Ivy's mother smiled and nodded. Amid many squeals, the girls grabbed their coats and shrugged into them, pulling scarves about their necks and hats over their ears. Ivy also went about the ritual of preparing to face the outside cold, but she did so more sedately than the girls.

Inside, her heart mocked her with its rapid beats.

Ivy met Craig at the door. "Hello," she said, feeling at a strange loss for words. She motioned to Gwen and Crystin, who appeared at her side. "My sisters are coming with us."

"Of course they can come." The smile he gave them was genuine. He bent down to scratch Old Rufus between the ears. "There's room, but you two children might have to snuggle close like fox cubs."

At this, Crystin giggled. To be on the safe side, Ivy

planned the seating arrangement so that the slight Crystin was sandwiched between her and Craig, and Gwen sat behind them. The ride to town was filled with the little girls' excited chatter and Craig's patient answers to their questions.

Due to the nasty weather, the schoolhouse wasn't crowded, but Ivy was surprised to see among the towns-folk there a family who owned a claim a few miles away. The Reverend Michaels was young with bushy red eye-brows, long sideburns that swept down his jaws, and a decidedly Irish accent. He had a way of spearing a person with his intense blue eyes, and his words were full of something that convicted Ivy's heart. The passages he read from 1 Corinthians about love seared her conscience, and she thought back to what her mother had read earlier.

Perhaps Ivy never had tried to exhibit Christian char-ity or goodwill toward anyone while living in Leaning Tree and only expected to be treated kindly by others. Yet had she truly expected even that? She wasn't sure what she'd expected; she'd been so angry with her mother and new stepfather those first few months after she'd moved here. Yet the anger had begun to subside at some point without her realizing it. When had that happened?

After the rousing service, which lasted all morning, the people visited. Winifred pulled Ivy aside and asked how her parents were. Ivy explained that her mother wasn't feeling well, and both Winifred and Bronwyn shared a smile. "It will soon pass," Winifred said. "Give her tea with mint. It has helped me." She blushed.

By their reactions and words, Ivy felt a stab of dread. Oh no. Her mother couldn't be in a family way!

"It is the way of things," Bronwyn said, her blue eyes wise. "She is still young and strong. She will be fine."

Ivy nodded, though inside she felt like a newly broken wheel cast aside from the stagecoach whose destination promised a better life. How could Mother do this to her? How could Ivy leave Leaning Tree now?

"Are you all right?" Craig asked when they returned to his sleigh. Both Gwen and Crystin ran ahead and jumped in back, leaving Ivy no choice but to sit beside Craig. She did so stiffly, and he pulled up the bristly fur lap robe over their legs. She shivered when his arm and leg inadvertently pressed against hers in the confined space.

"Cold?" He pulled the lap robe up farther before taking the reins.

The warmth surging through her blocked out most of the chill.

"How did you get this sleigh?" she asked, raising her voice above the wind that resulted from the vehicle's movement once it was in motion. If they talked about inconsequential matters, she might be able to concentrate on those issues and not on the man sitting so close to her.

"A customer asked me to fix it for him last year, but he ended up moving back East. When I reminded him about the sleigh before he left, he told me that if I could fix it, I could have it. It was in bad shape when he brought it to me. It had hit a tree, and the runners were twisted."

"Did you make the bells on the horse's harness, too?"

"My cousin did. He's a silversmith who I'm trying to convince to move here. He's considering it. The town is growing, and by this time next year, I'd be surprised if the population hasn't doubled. We even have our own doc now."

Doubt edging her mind, Ivy looked at the ramshackle town. Either Craig had high aspirations or she was blind.

"Still doubt that Leaning Tree amounts to much?" he asked.

She shrugged, deciding it best not to comment. When he didn't steer the sleigh left at the turnoff leading to her stepfather's soddy, Ivy looked at him. "Where are you taking me?"

"To a little piece of the future."

"Where?" Her brows shot upward.

"You'll see. Relax, Ivy. You did agree to an outing after the service, and we do have the girls along as chaperones."

Some chaperones. A glance over her shoulder revealed that Gwen and Crystin had their heads tucked underneath their lap robe. Occasionally, a giggle would escape from beneath the fur.

"All right. I suppose," she gave her grudging consent.

Craig steered the sleigh by a copse of trees growing along the stream. White coated any remaining leaves and branches, and the water lazily trickled under a thin crust of ice.

"See that?" Craig pointed to a tree whose trunk leaned at an angle toward the water. "That's how the town got its name."

Ivy was interested despite her resolve not to be. She'd never been in this area before. Where her stepfather lived, there wasn't a tree in sight, though a scant few grew on the outskirts of town. She'd recently heard her stepfather and Winifred's husband discuss a man named J. Sterling Morton, who'd proposed an idea for everyone in Nebraska to plant a tree next spring. He felt the economy would benefit from the wide-scale planting. Ivy looked over the vast land of untouched white that the sleigh now faced. It would take a great many trees to make that happen! She tried to imagine all that empty white being broken up by forests of trees or even a small wood.

"What do you see?" Craig's soft voice caught her attention.

What did she see? "Um, snow, and a lot of land. Gray skies above."

"Know what I see?" She shook her head, and he continued, "I see opportunity. A land that's ready for growth and is just waiting to be farmed or used in other ways for the good of the community, even the nation. Miles and miles of rich, fertile soil ready for the first touch of that plow."

She turned her head to look at him. "Are you planning to trade in your anvil and become a farmer?"

He chuckled. "No. But where there are farming tools, mules, and horses, there's a need for a blacksmith. And where there's virgin land, there's a need for people with enough courage to carve out a promising future. People who won't say no to a challenge, who keep on when all they want to do is quit." His gaze briefly swept the land again. "And I believe you're one of those people, Boston. I believe you've got what it takes."

Ivy jerked in surprise. "Surely, you're teasing me."

"No. You've got gumption. I noticed that the first day we met. While it's true you weren't happy to come here and felt forced into it, you made do and adjusted the best you could. I have a feeling that if you'd also adjust your thinking and try to see some good in this town, you might find that this could be more of a home to you than Boston ever was."

"I sincerely doubt that."

He shrugged. "Just don't close your mind to the possibility. It may be that you coming here was all part of God's plan."

His words irritated her, and she looked away to the sweeping vista. "Please take me home, Mr. Watson."

"Don't you think you could learn to call me Craig?"

"Only if you'll stop calling me Boston!" The words shot out of her mouth before she could stop them.

Craig laughed, a rich, exuberant sound that warmed her clear through and brought two small heads from beneath the fur lap robe. "I can't promise I'll always remember," he said. "But I like the name Ivy, so I'll surely try."

That wasn't what she'd meant—she'd meant for him to address her properly by her surname. She opened her mouth to tell him so, then snapped it shut. Oh, what was the use? From what she knew of the man, Craig Watson would likely do as he pleased. Moreover, she did notice that the people in Leaning Tree weren't big on formality. So maybe no one would make anything of it.

Another pair of giggles brought her sharp focus to the girls, who quickly ducked their heads back underneath the blanket.

Ivy watched her mother pull the flat iron from the top of the cookstove and continue to press the wrinkles out of Gavin's shirt. She turned back to her own task of kneading bread dough. Since Winifred and Bronwyn had spoken to her after Reverend Michael's message three weeks ago, Ivy had kept a close eye on her mother. Mama hadn't told her she was expecting, but that was little surprise. Such things weren't discussed in polite society, and her mother had been raised in Boston, too. What had happened to make Mama forget that? Why would she wish to leave behind a life filled with every luxury imaginable to marry a poor farmer?

At the other end of the table, Crystin painstakingly used a pencil nub to write out a short essay on the discarded brown paper that had been wrapped around a parcel from the general store. By the light of a kerosene lamp, Gwen read the book on colonial life her teacher had lent her. Outside, the night was still and not as cold as it had been. December proved to be milder than Ivy expected, with few scattered snows. Yet she'd been warned that January had the teeth of a wolf—and being snowbound for days or weeks wasn't an improbability.

"What are you working on so diligently, Crystin?" Ivy's mother asked.

Crystin looked up from her paper. "We must write an essay on what we like most about Christmas and then tell what's most important." She looked in the direction of the sleeping quarters of the two-room soddy. "Will we go to Aunt Winifred's and pull taffy, Dada?"

Gavin walked into the room and sat at the opposite end of the table. He pulled a handmade pipe from his mouth and turned his blue eyes to his youngest daughter. "Much will depend on the weather."

"I hope we do," Crystin said wistfully. "That's one of the things I like best about Christmas."

"I like the *Mari Lwyd*," Gwen said, putting down her book. She turned her gaze toward Ivy, who stood less than a foot away. "That's where a big horse's skull knocks on your door to ask a question, and if you get it wrong. . ." She mashed her elbows together, hands wide apart, then brought her palms to connect with a loud smack directed Ivy's way. Startled, Ivy jumped.

"Snap!" Gwen continued gleefully, a smug look in her eye. "Off with your head."

"Gwendolyn, I will have no more of such foolish talk,"

her father said sternly. "Or perhaps you shall not get the pink sugar mouse in your stocking this Christmas. You are too young to remember the customs practiced in the old country."

"Did the horse's skull really bite people's heads off?" Crystin's eyes were wide.

"No." Gavin directed another severe look at Gwen before explaining. "The *Mari Lwyd* was an ancient ritual for luck the townsfolk played among one another, a game of wits. No one was hurt."

"What is your favorite Christmas memory, Dada?" Crystin asked.

Gavin's eyes grew misty. "I remember going with my brother, Dai, to the *Plygain,* since the time we were young men. It is a service where the townsmen sing carols and songs and read from the Bible. Always, it takes place in the dark hours of Christmas morning before the dawn."

"While the women pull taffy!" Crystin inserted eagerly. "Nana told me that."

"Yes." Gavin's word came softly. He stared into the distance, and Ivy wondered if he was thinking about his brother.

"What about you, Ivy?" Crystin suddenly asked. "What's your favorite thing about Christmas?"

Ivy stopped kneading the dough, surprised the child

would ask but heartened that she had. She thought back to happier Christmases. "In Boston my grandmother gives a festive party and a grand ball during the Christmas season. Everyone of importance is invited, from the mayor to the wealthy ship merchants to the doctors and their families. People come from miles around to enjoy one of her affairs. There's dancing until all hours of the night and lavish banquets with roast goose and plum pudding. Among the many pastries she has her chef make are lady fingers, since she knows how much I fancy them."

Crystin looked horrified. "You eat ladies' fingers?"

Ivy shared a smile with her mother. "They are thin white cookies the size of a woman's finger. That's how they got their name, I suppose. You dip them in chocolate, or they have chocolate spread over them. I've eaten them both ways."

"A cookie with white sugar? I can't remember the last time I had white sugar."

"Brown sugar is just as good, Crystin," Gwen said, a sting in her voice. She ducked her head back toward her book before her father could see, but the look she shot Ivy spoke volumes.

Ivy knew the white variety was expensive because it was scarce. Most settlers used brown sugar instead. Seeing Crystin's wistful expression, Ivy wished she hadn't spoken.

She pounded the dough, placed it in a pan, then covered it with a towel and left it near the warmth of the stove to rise. Thankfully, this time she hadn't forgotten the yeast. Last time she'd made bread, her thoughts had been centered on Craig instead of the contents she mixed in the bowl, and she had omitted that most essential ingredient. Gwen had teased her mercilessly about her flat bread, and Ivy had bitten her tongue so as not to respond sharply.

She recalled the last time she'd seen Craig, in late November when he'd taken her for another ride in his sleigh before that first snow melted to mush. He'd told her then that he also had a stepmother and stepsister, and adjustments had been difficult for him, too, at first. None of them were able to get along, so he could sympathize with Ivy's plight.

Then he'd said something to make her think. He told her that one day his stepsister went missing. During the search, Craig realized he didn't actually want her gone, as he'd often thought after one of their rows. The dread he'd felt until they found her safe in the tall grasses helped to dissolve the distance between them, and he was able to open his heart and see that his stepmother and stepsister weren't quite so bad as he'd thought. In fact, according to Craig, they had formed a caring relationship before the women had moved with his father farther west to California.

Ivy wondered why Craig hadn't also gone but was glad he'd decided to stay. To her amazement, she'd found him good company.

Ivy looked at Gwen and Crystin. They could be a trial at times, especially Gwen, but Ivy wouldn't wish evil upon either of them. Again, memory of Craig's words during that first sleigh ride revisited her—that if she would only adjust her thinking, she might find some good in Leaning Tree. Ivy pondered the idea and recalled the past months of living on the prairie.

She hadn't been fond of the inch-long worms that appeared on the walls, ceiling, and floor after a hard rain months ago. Nor did she like the dirt that sifted down and once landed in her bowl of fried corn mush. And she detested the snakes that liked to hide in tall grasses—and the one that preferred the soddy this past summer and had suddenly dropped down from the inside wall, landed at the foot of her cot, and frightened her silly. She had jumped out of bed and run outside screaming, while Gwen had doubled over laughing. Still, Ivy had to admit that the little sod house stayed warmer in winter and cooler in summer than a wooden one, and since her stepfather had plastered and whitewashed the inside walls, the place even seemed somewhat cheerful.

She enjoyed the huge canopy of sky that was often a rich, robin's egg blue and stretched on endlessly without any buildings or trees to mar it. Wildflowers in spring dressed the grass with abundant splashes of crimson, gold, and purple, pleasing to the eye. And when she stood outside and looked in all four directions at the miles of wind-swept grassland, an exhilarating feeling of freedom sometimes surged through her.

That was the sole thing about Boston that Ivy didn't like. Sometimes she'd felt confined. Here, anytime she felt the need to leave the cramped soddy, she could walk outside for miles with nothing but the constant, whispering wind for company—and Old Rufus, when the hound chose to trot beside her. The hard work that resulted from living on the prairie and all the walking she'd done had trimmed her figure and given her muscles a strength they'd never before had. Town wasn't so far away that she couldn't visit, and often she did, though she had yet to make friends. Unless she could count Craig Watson as a friend. . .

A rush of warmth tingled through Ivy, and she attributed it to standing so near the cookstove. She stepped over to the window and parted the curtains made of flour sacks embroidered with green flowers. A thick frost covered the ground, and a half moon provided little light. She might not want to admit it, but she was growing accustomed to living in this place.

"Gwen, Crystin, come with me to tend the animals," Ivy's stepfather suddenly said.

"Yes, Dada," they both replied.

Once the three left the soddy with Old Rufus trotting beside them, Ivy watched their trek to a smaller soddy that her stepfather had made to house the cow, the horse, and the chickens in winter.

"Ivy, a word with you." Mother's soft voice bore a trace of sobriety, and Ivy knew she must have signaled Gavin to leave with the children so that the two of them could speak privately. She turned to face her mother.

"I know life has been difficult for you here and that you miss Boston a great deal," her mama began. She sat down on the bench and laid one work-worn hand over the other on the table, then stared at them. "To understand why I wouldn't allow you to stay with your grandmother, as you asked of me, I would have to recall the past and speak of issues I long to forget. Suffice it to say, my mother and I had opposing views as to what was important, and I didn't want you under her sole influence."

Ivy took a seat across the table, waiting for her to go on.

"I love my mother, but we see things differently. She

wasn't pleased when I married your father. She wanted me to wed someone wealthier, though your father wasn't poor. When he died, I was devastated and chose to move in with her. You were only six at the time."

Ivy knew this already but nodded in acknowledgment.

"Wealth and position are of paramount importance to my mother. It's true that I enjoyed many luxuries while growing up in my parents' home, but your father helped me to see that there were more important matters in life, such as God and family." Her mother reached across to take hold of Ivy's hand. "I wanted you to learn this, too. Your father would have wanted it."

"I know, Mama," Ivy said, her voice a wisp.

"You will soon be seventeen," her mother said. "A woman of marriageable age. I know I cannot keep you with me forever if you wish to go, but I ask that you remain here until early summer. You see," a faint blush touched her face, "I am expecting and will need your help. Mother Morgan told me that you knew."

Ivy looked at her lap and nodded. She'd never spoken of that first telegram she'd sent to Grandmother but wondered if Mama might have somehow learned of it. Once Ivy found out about her mother's delicate condition, she'd sent another telegram, this one telling her grandmother that she would have to delay her travel plans until after the baby came.

"I only want what's best for you, Ivy, and I considered it best to bring you with us to Nebraska. I wanted us to be a family. If I erred in that respect, forgive me. I don't want us to drift apart as Gavin and his brother have done."

Ivy's head snapped up. "Oh no, Mama!" She moved off the bench to hug her mother. "I could never feel any ill will toward you. I know that you love me."

Her mother smoothed Ivy's hair, much as she had done when Ivy was a child. "I spoke to you of this because you're old enough to understand such matters now. You've matured in the months we've lived here, and I thought it time that you know the lay of things. However, your grandmother loves you as well, Ivy. It is not my wish for you to bear any ill feelings toward her."

"I don't, Mama." Ivy thought about the money her grandmother had given her with explicit instructions not to tell her mother. Grandmother often did things like that, allowing Ivy to have anything she wanted against her mother's wishes and without her knowledge. As Ivy grew older, she'd felt uneasy about the duplicity. Perhaps she should tell Mother of the fifty dollars.

"Well, then!" her mother exclaimed, her voice light, signaling an end to the serious discussion. "If I'm to learn how to make a pink sugar mouse, I must find a way to do so with the ingredients I have. I shall make one tonight once the girls are asleep."

Ivy pulled away. "A pink sugar mouse?"

"A Welsh custom. I don't want Gwen and Crystin to be disappointed on Christmas morning when they look into their stockings."

"Can't Winifred or her mother do it, since they likely know how and we plan to be at their house on Christmas Eve?"

"Winifred has enough to do preparing for the social that she plans to hold for anyone who will come. It will be the last gathering before she turns her home into a boardinghouse this spring."

"Still, Christmas is a week away."

"Yes, but I need the practice. I've never made anything remotely like a sugar mouse." Her mother smiled. "Will you help me?"

"But, Mama, you know I haven't yet learned to cook without burning what I do make!"

"I know. Yet this can be something we learn together. We can help one another. Mother Morgan told me some of how it's done, but I've no idea how to make the mouse pink! Berry juice from preserves perhaps? What do you think?"

Ivy smiled. "That might work." Suddenly she felt

lighthearted and looked forward to the event. Who would have thought the idea of making a pink sugar mouse with her mother could give her such joy?

"Will all the townspeople come to Winifred's on Christmas Eve?" she asked.

"All have been invited. Whether they will come or not is another matter." A gleam lit her mother's eye. "Was there anyone in particular you were inquiring after?"

Ivy rose from the bench to sort through the freshly pressed laundry and collect her things. "Of course not." Yet when thoughts of Craig visited, she realized that wasn't entirely true.

Chapter 5

Christmas Eve arrived cold and windy with a few inches of new snow. Yet the weather wasn't bad enough for Gavin to cancel their outing to his sister's place. They bundled up for the ride in the wagon. Before they could leave the soddy, Old Rufus barked and ran to the door. Soon the jingling of bells alerted them to company. Ivy hurried to the window to see, as did Gwen and Crystin.

"It's Craig, and he's in his sleigh!" Crystin announced.

Gwen threw open the door. "Hulloa!"

For a moment, Craig seemed uncertain. "Hello. I came to ask permission to take Ivy to the social."

Ivy felt her face warm while her stepfather seemed to mull over the request. From the twinkle in his eyes, Ivy wondered if this was the first he'd known about Craig's invitation. "I think you'd best ask Ivy," Gavin instructed.

"Ivy?" Craig looked her way, his brown eyes hopeful. "Will you accompany me?"

She hesitated, not wanting to seem too eager, then nodded and walked toward his sleigh. She did enjoy his company, even if considering him for a husband was out of the question. Instantly he scrambled from the conveyance to help her into it.

"Can we go, too, Dada?" Ivy heard Crystin ask from behind.

"Not this time. There is a pout; now then, I'll have none of it," he said a little more sternly. "Or you will have no taffy pulling this night."

"Oh no, Dada, I'll be good," Crystin hurried to say.

As though afraid he might indeed change his mind, both Gwen and Crystin scampered in the direction of the wagon, which sat hitched up and waiting by the barn. Gavin chuckled and nodded to both Craig and Ivy before he and Ivy's mother set off in that direction.

The sleigh whizzed over the snow the short two miles to Winifred's, while the wagon bumped over small drifts at a much slower pace. Ivy noticed that the Bradfords' wagon was coming from the east, from the direction of their claim, and also headed toward town. All sixteen of the Bradfords appeared to be packed inside.

"I'm surprised they're taking the time to go to something like this," Ivy mused.

"A social is good enough reason for everyone to put off work for a few hours," Craig explained. "They're few and far between, especially this time of year. I worked extra hard this week at the smithy getting orders filled so that I would have today to enjoy with my neighbors."

Despite the chill air blowing on parts of her face not covered by the woolen scarf, Ivy's skin and insides warmed with embarrassment. She hadn't reckoned on Craig hearing her observation about the Bradfords. The man must have the hearing of a hound! Yet she was glad that he would be there—just as a friend, of course. Ivy certainly had no other reason for desiring his company.

Sleigh bells ringing, they soon arrived at the white timbered house. A curl of gray smoke rose into the sky from the chimney. Craig took care of the horse and sleigh, while Ivy hurried up the wooden steps. Thankfully, they weren't coated in ice.

Winifred met her at the door. "Hello, Ivy. I'm glad you could make it! But. . ." Her brow creased, and she looked behind Ivy in the direction of the road. "Where are my brother, your mother, and my nieces?"

"They took the wagon. Craig brought me." Too late, she realized the slip of using his first name in public.

Winifred smiled. "Come in and get warm."

Ivy did so, though she left her cloak on. It was cold inside even with the fire to warm the parlor. From what Ivy knew, the Pettigrasses were the only people in Leaning Tree to own a genuine parlor, but then, Winifred's husband was wealthy, though not as wealthy as Ivy's grandmother. As Ivy drew nearer to the blaze, she noticed wood didn't burn there but the usual "Nebraska coal," as her stepfather chose to call the cow refuse. She looked toward the corner where someone had chopped down a wild plum bush to use as a Christmas tree and had decorated it with strings of popcorn.

"Greetings, Ivy," Bronwyn said, coming from another room, a fine china cup and saucer in her hand. "Have some wassail to warm yourself." She offered the steaming cup to Ivy, who gratefully took a short sip. Piping hot apple, cloves, and cinnamon teased her tongue while delicious warmth filled her.

The door constantly opened as more people arrived. A few were Welsh immigrants who'd also settled in Leaning Tree like the Morgans. It appeared that everyone who lived nearby was making a showing, and the parlor soon felt cramped and warm. Men and women talked and visited. Older children rushed outdoors to amuse themselves, while the younger girls sat in a circle to play with the corncob dolls they'd brought from home.

As the afternoon progressed, some of the families left the gathering early. Mrs. Llewynn's husband, Milton, brought out his fiddle, and lively music filled the place. A few men, including Craig, circled the baldheaded fiddle player. They clapped their hands and stomped their feet to the frenetic melody while the women flocked together and chattered away like magpies who hadn't seen each other for an entire season. The topic was the second theft of one of Mrs. Llewynn's chickens just that morning.

"Well," Mrs. Johnson, the feed store owner's wife, said, "I think it's just horrendous. And on Christmas Eve, besides. Whoever would do such a thing? A definite ill-bred churl, if you ask me." Her gaze speared Mrs. Bradford, and Ivy felt the look was deliberate. Did Rowena Johnson suspect one of the Bradford children of being a chicken thief?

"I'll be thankful when we get a sheriff for this town," Mrs. Llewynn said. "As well as a preacher." Suddenly she was all smiles. "I hear, dear Winifred, that the men of Leaning Tree asked your husband to act as our first mayor."

"Yes," Winifred said. "It is all so exciting."

"Then he has agreed?" the doctor's wife, Adella Miller, asked.

Ivy's attention was diverted to Bronwyn, who offered each of the guests their choice from a platter layered with fancy iced cookies and sliced fruitcake. Ivy had never seen Crystin's eyes go so round as they did when her grandmother held out the tray toward her. The child moved her small hand in the air over each item, as though uncertain of which to take, then opted for a slice of fruitcake. Ivy took a cookie. It was brittle, but it wasn't bad.

"Your mother tells me of the pink sugar mouse and your attempts to make one for my granddaughters," Bronwyn said, eyes twinkling.

Ivy felt the blush rise to her face and was thankful no one was within hearing distance. Crystin had taken her cake and moved toward one of the Bradford children. "Yes, and sad attempts they were, too. They crumbled to nothing."

Bronwyn chuckled. "Tonight, after the girls sleep, I will show you both how it is done. Pleased I am that your mama tries so hard to be a good mother to Gwendolyn and Crystin. The Lord smiled the day Gavin met your mama. Before she came, lonely were the girls to have no mother."

Ivy saw the truth of what the elderly woman said, though her poetic way of speaking was a bit difficult to follow at times. Ivy's mother was kind and unselfish, wanting only the best for her family. She had adapted to this wild prairie life and was a good wife to Gavin, too.

"It is also well to have you as part of our family, Ivy," Bronwyn continued. "There is kind, you are, to be a good sister to the girls. To you as an example they look."

If Ivy wasn't well trained in social etiquette, she might have gawked or allowed her cup to clatter to the saucer. Gwen definitely didn't regard her as a friend!

Bronwyn seemed to read her thoughts. "Gwendolyn is like my youngest son, Dai. Stubborn he is, with a strong will. The voyage to America and losing her mother years later to fever made troubles for Gwendolyn. She was made to tend Crystin much, and she, only a child herself. She is angry but does not dislike you. Many times I see her watch and imitate what you do. As she does now." Bronwyn smiled and barely nodded to a corner of the room.

Ivy's gaze followed. Gwen stood, adopting the same well-postured stance as Ivy, with her little finger in the air as she sipped her tea and smiled politely at those nearby.

Suddenly Ivy heard raised voices, and she looked to see that the Bradfords were leaving. Mr. Bradford, his face flushed, said something to Wesley. The boy grabbed the hand of one of his young brothers and hurried outside. Two of his sisters followed. Had Mrs. Bradford been offended by Mrs. Johnson's remark or the taciturn look she'd given? She didn't look happy. Nor did Mr. Bradford.

Bronwyn rushed toward the couple to offer her fare-wells, Ivy assumed. As the front door swung open, she noticed that the sky had grown murky and a heavy snow fell. The Johnsons and another couple gathered their outer wraps, making for home as well.

"Will you also need to leave since the weather's taken a turn for the worse?" Craig's voice came from near her elbow.

Ivy managed to keep her grip on the saucer, though her cup gave a telltale clatter. She hadn't heard him come up beside her. Perhaps there was a disadvantage to having a carpet cover the floor.

"No," she said. "My mother and sisters and I plan to stay and take part in the late-night taffy pulling. My step-father will return to the soddy to tend the animals. He'll come back for us in the morning."

Craig nodded. "I imagine this isn't anything like the fancy socials you're used to. But admit it, Ivy—you did have a good time today, didn't you?"

Why his words should irk her so, especially since there was a ring of truth to them, she didn't know. She raised her chin a notch. "Why should you think that?"

"Because your cheeks are glowing like summer-ripe strawberries, and your eyes are sparkling like blueberries after the rain." His grin was teasing, his gaze admiring.

Ivy felt the hot blush spread toward her ears and down her neck. She lowered her voice to a whisper so only Craig could hear. "If my face is glowing and my eyes are shining, it's due to annoyance regarding your improper behavior, Mr. Watson. Kindly desist from further talk of comparing my features to fruit."

Craig let out a loud laugh, bringing a few glances their way. He shook his head, still grinning. "Boston, you are the only woman I know to get offended by a compliment. But in the future, I'll keep your wishes in mind."

"Miss Ivy." A child's voice spoke to her right.

Ivy swung her gaze in surprise to see Amy Bradford standing there.

"Do you know where my mama is?"

Alarm filled Craig as he looked at Amy, whose tousled golden hair and heavy-lidded eyes suggested she'd been sleeping. "I was hidin' from Wesley, but he never came and found me. I don't see none of my family here, neither."

Craig quickly bridged the distance to the door and opened it. Behind him the fiddle playing stopped. The wind blew the snow harder, and some of it swirled inside. He could see the Bradfords' wagon in the distance, slowly making its way home. He closed the door and strode to the fireplace. Winifred had joined Ivy, who had an arm around the girl's shoulders. Amy now looked wide-awake, her eyes uncertain and a little afraid. Apparently she'd just learned that she'd been left behind—again. Why the Bradfords couldn't keep track of their children, Craig didn't understand. Fourteen kids was a lot for any couple, but this kind of situation happened far too often to be called accidental. More like negligent.

He hunkered down in front of the child and smiled. "Ever ride in a sleigh, Amy?"

She shook her head no.

"Would you like to? We can catch up to your folks in no time."

Her eyes began to shine. "You mean that sleigh with all those pretty ringin' bells? Oh yes, Mr. Watson. I'd like that awful much."

"Then let's hurry."

While Craig shrugged into his outerwear, Ivy buttoned Amy's threadbare coat, which looked a size too small. "Is this all you have to wear, Amy? Have you no hat or scarf?"

The girl shook her head.

"I'll just go upstairs and get a quilt to wrap her up in," Winifred offered.

The wind raised its voice, an angry foe, and now

Craig could hear it shrieking through the eaves. "Better make it fast, ma'am. I want to get back before the weather gets worse."

"You think it will?" Ivy asked, concern edging her voice. "Are you certain you should risk it then? I'm sure Amy's parents will know that she's here and safe with us."

He grinned. "You worried about me, Boston?"

"Me worried? About you?" Pink stained her cheeks. "I've never heard of anything so vain. Why would you think such a thing? My concern was solely for Amy."

He chuckled. "Methinks the lady doth protest too much," he teased under his breath so Amy couldn't hear. "Shakespeare. *Hamlet.* And yes, I can read, too."

The pink swept up to cover Ivy's entire face. Winifred returned with the quilt, and Ivy quickly claimed it, kneeling down to wrap the child inside. "Merry Christmas, Amy. Mr. Watson will see that you get to your family safely."

"Thank you, Miss Ivy," the little girl whispered.

"I'll be back shortly," Craig said to Ivy. Maybe he shouldn't have teased her, but he hadn't meant the words in a negative way. He had only positive feelings with regard to Ivy. Yet he was beginning to wonder if she would ever feel anything for him. Eight months of trying to win her favor was a long time. Maybe such an effort really was wasted, as he'd been told often enough, and he should just give up.

Craig bent to scoop the bundled child in his arms. He could feel her tremble against him.

"Still cold?" he asked as he headed for the door.

"No. I'm just hopin' Pa won't be mad about this fix I'm in."

"It'll turn out all right. It wasn't your fault you got left behind." Sensing that she was still upset, he added, "Know what I do when I'm nervous or scared?"

"Pray to God to make it all better?"

"That, too. I also whistle. It relaxes me. Shall we whistle?"

She grinned and nodded. Yet as they stepped outside, the angry wind snatched their cheerful notes from their pursed lips, and Craig fought the wintry beast all the way to the sleigh.

Staring out the window at a world of white, Ivy stood with folded arms and rubbed them. Craig had left with Amy some time ago. Not long after his sleigh took off in the direction of the Bradfords' homestead, the wind increased to gale force, whipping snow first one way and then the other. Only for periodic snatches of time had Ivy been able to see farther than a few feet past the porch. A short time ago, the storm calmed some, though the snow still blew in whirls. At least she could see for a much greater distance than before.

Why had she snubbed Craig yet again when he'd asked her if she was worried about him? True, she'd been embarrassed that he'd so accurately discerned her thoughts. Regardless, she shouldn't have treated him so shamefully.

"Ivy, come away from that window," her mother gently commanded.

Ivy turned. "He should have been back by now."

"Perhaps he went home. The smithy is only across the road."

"No, he told me he'd be back shortly. Something's happened; I just know it." She glanced toward the window again, as if by doing so she could summon Craig back.

"Worrying won't help matters, dearest. All it will do is put wrinkles in that pretty forehead of yours. Now come here and let's pray."

Ivy did so, and her mother took her ice-cold hands in her own. "Father, we ask that You protect all Thy children out there. Help everyone to reach safety, and—"

Her mother's prayer was cut off as Ivy's stepfather and Winifred's husband walked into the room. Doc Miller and

Mr. Llewynn were right behind them. All the men wore coats, hats, and mufflers. "We've talked it over, and we're going to look for them," Gavin explained quietly. "There is no way the Bradfords could have reached home in time. And Craig cannot have gotten far."

Ivy's mother rose to hug Gavin, and Bronwyn did the same to her husband. Mrs. Llewynn wrapped the scarf a second time around her husband's neck and fussed with his coat. Then they watched the men walk outside into the dancing snow. Ivy moved to stand beside her mother and slipped her hand into hers, both to take comfort and give encouragement. "Heavenly Father," she said, taking up the prayer where her mother had left off and trying not to let her voice shake, "we earnestly ask that Thou wouldst be a guiding light and protect our husbands and fathers and friends so that they may find and help any who are in need."

Ivy's mother squeezed her hand. "Amen," she whispered.

Chapter 6

Minutes after Craig left the Pettigrasses, the blizzard had started in earnest. Though he wore thick gloves, he had ceased feeling his hands long ago. The unforgiving wind whipped stinging particles into his eyes, the only part of his face exposed to the blinding snow. He couldn't tell if the constant, faint ringing he heard was in his head or from the sleigh bells. The wind drowned out most other sounds. He should have listened to Ivy. If he had, Amy would be safe by the fire right now instead of curled up in fear under the lap robe beside him.

If only he could sense direction; if only he could see something around him besides a curtain of white. He hadn't driven that far before the storm worsened, so he'd turned back in what he assumed was the direction of town. Now they were struggling against the wind.

Father, my own stupidity got me into this mess. I was so sure I could beat the storm. Please don't let a little child's life be lost because of me. Show me where to go.

Traveling blindly on in a foreign world of nothing but white, Craig urged the horse forward. If they stopped, the horse might freeze. He might freeze. With that thought, he moved his limbs to try to keep the blood flowing while taking care not to drop the reins. Amy's thin arms suddenly clutched him tight around his waist. He couldn't blame her for being scared.

"Help, please."

Craig blinked. Did his ears deceive him? Had that been a human cry for help? He strained to hear against the forceful wind.

"Help."

Sensing the call was coming from his right, Craig directed the horse that way. He pulled down his muffler from his mouth. "Call again so I can find you." The wind snatched his words from him the second they reached the air, and he doubted he could be heard.

"Over here!" The reply came, stronger this time.

A shift in the wind made the dancing snow seem to stop and swerve. In that instant, Craig spotted a sod house with light coming from inside. He remembered it as belonging to a family who'd moved back East two summers ago after a prairie fire destroyed their crops.

Craig guided the sleigh less than a foot from where a boy stood in the open doorway. A lamp glowed inside the rundown one-room house, devoid of all furniture except for a small bed and table. Craig questioned the intelligence of leaving Amy in the sleigh, even for a short time, but he didn't know what he would find when he entered the soddy.

"I hear the bells and know help has come." A boy of perhaps eleven with shoulder-length black hair, brown skin, and liquid-dark eyes looked up at him. "Please to help my mama," he implored in broken English. "She very sick."

Craig stepped inside. No fire burned, though a flame steadily shone in the lamp's glass globe. Chicken feathers littered the earthen floor and table, and what was left of a stew sat in a pot. Craig would guess that he'd just discovered the identity of the chicken thief. Across the room a smaller boy sat on the cot, upon which a young woman lay stretched out, fully clothed. A baby nestled beside her.

"I am Roberto, and that is my brother, Paulo," the boy at the door said. "Mama sick many days, since my sister, Carmelita, come two months ago."

"Where is your father?" Craig asked.

"He died when we come west. We find this place, me

and Mama, and stay here now."

Craig moved forward. "Are you all right, ma'am?"

The huge, dark eyes of the beauty surveyed him, but she didn't answer.

"Mama speak no English."

"How is it that you do?"

Roberto smiled. "Boys in wagon train teach me some. Other words I learn after we leave our band."

Gypsies. That explained it.

"And did you learn to steal chickens, too?"

The boy's eyes glittered in defense. "The store owner has many birds. My mother and brother are hungry. I am head of family now." He puffed his small chest out. "My duty is to feed them."

Craig decided this wasn't the time for reprimands. Realizing the situation wasn't dangerous, he went to collect Amy from the sleigh. Roberto's eyes widened when he saw the girl in Craig's arms, and his fascinated gaze focused on her snow-covered fair hair. Craig set Amy down, shut the door, and searched for fuel to make a fire. He must get the place warm. Then he would figure out what to do next.

"Put a table by the front window," Bronwyn ordered a

few minutes after the storm worsened and the wind increased again. "Fill it with every candle and lamp in the house. Do the same with the upstairs window, Winifred."

Her directives caused the women to hurry into action. Soon a yellow blaze lit up the rattling pane from the inside, and the aroma of honey from many beeswax candles filled the room. The rest of the house was dim, but if sacrificing light with which to see might help bring the men home safely, Ivy wasn't going to complain.

She prayed nonstop for Craig and the Bradfords, for the search party, and for her stepfather. She was surprised that she felt so strongly about her stepfather's safety and realized she didn't dislike him at all. Now that she was being honest with herself, she silently admitted that she approved of her mother's husband even though he had chosen to make his home on the prairie. He took care of Ivy and never ceased to treat her as one of his daughters despite how she behaved. She burned with shame when she thought of the caustic remarks she'd flung his way upon her arrival in Nebraska. He wasn't her own dear papa, but he was a good man, a strong man, and he obviously loved her mother. Ivy owed him her respect.

When her thoughts returned to Craig, she forced her hands to any task that presented itself to help her forget. She couldn't think of him right now or she might cry. It had taken a blizzard to make her realize she loved the man. She didn't know what she would do if Craig were killed, if she never saw his sunny smile or heard his warm, teasing words again. How she wished she could retrieve every occasion on which she'd acted indifferently toward him or ignored him outright.

As they waited, Bronwyn took the chair beside Ivy and began to speak of her son Gavin and of how proud she was of what he'd achieved. Her reminiscences brought up the conflict between Gavin and his brother, something about which Ivy often wondered. Ivy's heart ached for the brothers and their mother, who felt torn by the anger between sons. Gavin, the oldest, strongly felt the responsibility for his family and had worked hard to keep them together. Upon reaching America, his brother had other ideas. Gavin assumed Dai would help him stake his claim during the five years necessary to possess the land, but Dai had not wanted to be a farmer. Harsh words arose between them, ending in fisticuffs, before Dai stalked off, angry. That had been seven years ago, and to this day, Gavin and Dai had not seen one another or written to each other.

"I pray for them, every night, to end their quarrel," Bronwyn admitted, tears trickling freely from her eyes. "I miss my Dai. There it is. Only the Almighty can work in my sons' stubborn hearts."

Ivy thought about Bronwyn's words as she took her mother some tea with mint. "Winifred said this will help ease the sickness, and it might help to calm your nerves, too."

Her mother took the saucer. Ivy noticed how her hand trembled and the small amount of liquid that sloshed from the teacup.

"Mama, please don't be upset. We've prayed, and now we must trust. We mustn't worry, as you said. My step-father is an intelligent man; I've seen this. He's not one to make foolhardy decisions."

Her mother laid a palm against Ivy's cheek. "Bless you, dearest. Thank you for being such a comfort to me."

Ivy took her mother's hand—a hand that had once been so smooth and pale but was now rough and brown—and kissed the inside of her callused fingers. Then she moved around the room to serve tea to the other women. She found that she enjoyed helping by doing what she could; it gave her a sense of purpose and helped to keep her thoughts off Craig.

"Ivy," Winifred said, "in the spring when the weather warms, the women will meet for a quilting bee each week. We would like for you to join us."

"Thank you, but I don't know how to quilt." She felt embarrassed to admit it.

"We will teach you," Winifred said with a faint smile. "It will be a time for us to encourage and pray for one another's needs also. As we are doing this day," she said more softly.

Ivy felt tears prick her eyes at the sense of unity she suddenly felt toward these women. "I'd like that."

"Listen!" Adella Miller lifted her head of tight curls higher. "Do I hear bells?"

"It must be Craig!" Forgetting etiquette, Ivy set the platter holding the tea pitcher down with a bang and rushed to the door, throwing it open. The snow didn't swirl as heavily. The icy wind sucked the breath from her lungs, but its effect didn't compare to the breathlessness she felt at the sight of a sleigh drawing closer.

"Craig," she whispered, clutching the doorframe.

He awkwardly exited the conveyance and picked up a long bundle. As he drew closer, Ivy could see he carried a woman. Amy and two other children hurried behind them, bent over as the wind half blew them to the porch.

"Hiya, B–Boston," Craig said stiffly from between blue lips as he moved across the threshold. "Miss me?"

The gripping emotion of wondering if he were dead, then seeing him alive—with a strange woman in his arms—was almost Ivy's undoing. She couldn't respond. She stared at him for a few quick heartbeats, then gave a

91

short, abrupt nod and switched her focus to Amy and the two boys.

Ivy helped to get the children out of their snow-encrusted coats, hats, and mufflers and noticed Bronwyn and Winifred doing the same for Craig. Ivy's mother and Adella were tending to the woman, whom Ivy could now see clutched a baby to her chest. Mrs. Llewynn took the child. When Ivy felt she could face Craig again, she shifted her gaze to where he'd taken a seat in a chair nearby. He was wrapped in a quilt, and icy particles of snow still clung to his eyebrows, hair, and eyelashes. His skin looked pale, his brown eyes serious.

"You really d–did miss me," he said, his words still stilted from the cold. They didn't contain any of their usual teasing but were filled with amazement.

"Drink your tea," she ordered, noticing that he held a cup someone had given him.

As he lifted the steaming cup to his blue lips, Ivy decided to be honest with him. After her telling actions upon his arrival, she couldn't very well pretend differently. Nor did she want to. "Yes, I did miss you. I was worried about you and continually prayed for you—and the others."

Craig frowned. "What others? The B–Bradfords?"

Ivy nodded. "And the men who went searching."

Craig clumsily set his cup and saucer on the floor. "I must help them."

To his obvious amazement—and hers—Ivy pushed him back in the chair with one hand. "Oh no, you mustn't! You might get lost again, out there all alone. Look at you! You resemble a walking snowman. And your teeth are still chattering. You must get warm before you can even think about going back out there. How ever did you find your way?" She switched the topic, hoping to detain him.

He drained his tea. Winifred appeared, quickly refilled his cup, and moved away again to tend to the woman. Craig then related to Ivy what had happened and how he'd found the gypsy family. "When the wind stopped blowing so strong, I kn—knew I had to get Juanita to the doc."

"Juanita?"

"Roberto's mother. I prayed I was d—doing the right thing and took the risk once the storm died d—down, figuring out which direction to go from their s—soddy. I knew that town was to the w—west. While I was still a ways off, I saw a light and was sure God was leading me home. That was a smart thing you women did, putting those c—candles and lamps in the windows."

"It was Bronwyn's idea." Ivy hesitated. "Is Roberto's father away? Is that why he didn't come?"

Craig took another large swig of tea. "He died on their journey west."

"Oh. Then Roberto's mother is a widow." Ivy glanced her way. The exotic-looking woman was wrapped in a colorful blanket and seated before the fire. The baby was nestled at her bosom. "She's quite lovely."

"Not as lovely as you."

Craig's low words sped up Ivy's heartbeat. She blinked his way. The steady look in his eyes sent warmth trickling through her, and suddenly she didn't mind the cold so much.

"Miss Ivy," Amy said, walking up to her. She still trembled. "Are my m—ma and p—pa going to be okay? And my brothers and sisters?"

Ivy hugged the girl close, rubbing her arm to help warm her. "We can pray that God will keep them safe, as we've been doing since this started." Noticing the concern on Gwen's and Crystin's faces as they kept casting glances toward the door and window, Ivy came up with a plan.

"Bronwyn, didn't you tell me that one of your traditions is to put on a Christmas play?"

"Yes, every year in the old country we hold a play of Christ's birth."

"Then let's have one now." Ivy ignored the shocked looks sent her way by the rest of the women. She thought that if they engaged in such a play, it might help lighten the atmosphere as they waited for their men to return.

Winifred looked at Ivy and nodded, lending her support. "Yes, this will be a good thing."

Ivy smiled her thanks at her stepfather's sister. "Amy, you be Mary. And Crystin, you can be the angel. Gwen, you shall be the wise man, since you're the eldest."

"Who will be Joseph?" Crystin asked.

Amy pulled on the older boy's arm. Ivy had noticed how he tried to edge out of the room during her announcement of the play. "Roberto can be Joseph—and we even have a baby to play Jesus!"

"But Carmelita's a girl!" Roberto protested.

"That's okay," Ivy assured him. "No one will be able to tell. If it's all right with you?" Ivy looked at Juanita for permission.

Roberto spoke in rapid Spanish to his mother. The woman looked mystified but nodded. She handed the baby to Roberto, then with another uncertain nod accepted the tea Winifred handed her.

"Perfect." Ivy smiled at her small cast of characters. "We shall need costumes."

Winifred smiled. "I will help. I have dresses I can no longer wear." She blushed, then hurried upstairs. Soon she returned, her arms full of ivory-, blue-, and peach-colored dresses, sheets, and a gold-topped walking stick that belonged to her husband. She handed the contributions to Ivy, then excused herself to make coffee.

Roberto folded his arms across his thin chest and absolutely refused to wear a sheet for his costume. However, he did accept the fancy walking stick to use for a staff. Crystin looked adorable in a white satin dress, though it was much too big for her; Winifred was petite like her mother, yet the dresses still hung on the girls.

Someone fashioned a "halo" from a ring of lace and set it atop Crystin's dark curls. Amy's thick, golden hair shone against the oversized, pale blue gown. The glow on her face and the brightness of her eyes as she stared at the baby in the manger—the cradle that would be used for Winifred's child—made her appear peaceful and awed, much like the Virgin Mary must have been. Ivy noticed how often Roberto stared Amy's way.

"Are we ready to begin?" Crystin asked. "Shall I make my announcement to the shepherd now?" The shepherd was Paulo, and he looked lost wrapped up in a white sheet with only his nut-brown face showing.

"Not quite," Ivy said. "There's one item we've overlooked." She undid the velvet ribbon from around her throat that held the garnet brooch and approached Gwen. "Why don't you wear this, since a king—or in this case a queen—would wear jewels?"

Gwen's mouth opened, but no words came out. Crystin gasped.

"Here," Ivy said, "I'll fasten it around your neck." Once she did, she stepped back to look. "Perfect." She smiled.

"Thank you," Gwen whispered, awkwardly fingering the square jewel and seed pearls.

The old irritation rose up, but Ivy squelched it. Her sister's fingerprints couldn't harm the brooch, nor could she hurt it if she squeezed the stone too hard. The truth was, Ivy had thought up that and any other ridiculous notion as an excuse to be selfish with her things. *Dear God, forgive me for being so self-centered*, she prayed when she saw Gwen's joy at wearing the brooch. The genuine smile the girl sent Ivy did her heart good. Perhaps they really could be friends someday.

The children began their rendition of Christ's birth. Roberto walked with Amy from the top of the stairs to the parlor to reenact the journey into Bethlehem. Carmelita gurgled from her place in the wooden cradle off to the side, awaiting her debut appearance.

"I am tired and hungry, Joseph," Amy said, putting one arm across her stomach and draping her other hand across her forehead. "I need rest."

"I will find us a chicken," Roberto proclaimed.

"That's not what you're supposed to say," Amy hissed.

Mrs. Llewynn raised her brows, and Craig leaned toward her. "I have something I need to tell you later," he whispered, the effects of the cold no longer affecting his speech.

"I think I know." The woman looked at the skinny boys, then at their sickly mother wrapped in quilts and leaning weakly back against her chair. A smile replaced Mrs. Llewynn's frown. "Never mind. I'm sure we can work this out to benefit everyone. I could use a strong boy like Roberto to help at the store. As you said, we will discuss this later."

Ivy decided that she also wished to discuss a matter with Mrs. Llewynn when she could get the woman alone—the purchase of a doll with a real china face for Crystin and of a leather-bound book of children's stories for Gwen. She remembered seeing such items in the general store. Add to that the beautiful oak cradle she'd also noticed—a cast-off from a family who'd returned back East—that would make a perfect gift for a new baby sister or brother. She should have enough of her fifty dollars left over to buy several yards of material for both her and her mother to have spring dresses. And gloves. She simply must buy herself new gloves.

Ivy mentally created her Christmas list. Hopefully

the gifts would impart the message she wished to convey: that she now considered them all her family.

"You look like the cat that got away with the mouse," Craig whispered to Ivy as Gwen, the wise man, moved forward bearing a plate with an iced cookie and a piece of fruitcake to use as a gift for the baby. Roberto eyed the offerings hungrily.

Ivy winced and glanced at Craig. "Please, don't talk to me about mice," she whispered. "Not after our failure with the pink Christmas mouse."

"That sounds like it could be an interesting story," he mused. "A pink Christmas mouse? Still, I have to wonder what would cause your face to glow like that, as if you'd just swallowed one of those candles. Pleased with yourself and the play, maybe? A great success, by the way. The women's minds are off their worries for the time being. And the children are having the time of their lives."

Ivy smiled. It was true. "I just came to the realization that this is where I belong. Being here finally feels right, as if I fit in now."

A couple of heartbeats passed before Craig spoke. "Ivy, look at me." His tone was serious.

She turned to stare into his steady brown eyes.

"Are you telling me that you've decided to stay in Leaning Tree?"

"Yes, Craig. This night has helped me to discover what's truly important, as well as shown me how foolish I've been."

Before she could explain further, the door blew open. Four white-crusted figures stiffly clomped inside, followed by fifteen more shivering forms.

"Ma!" Amy cried, abandoning her role when she caught sight of her mother. She almost tripped over the borrowed dress in her haste to get to her. The women jumped up from their chairs to embrace their frozen husbands and help them and the others out of icicle-laden coats and mufflers. Roberto dove for the slice of cake and crammed the entire thing into his mouth, his smile wide.

"It w—was a miracle we f—found the p—place before we f—froze to death," Ivy's stepfather said, his teeth chattering. "Their w—wagon was stuck. W—we had to w—walk, and I th—thought all w—was lost when the s—storm started up again. Then, w—we saw that light in the w—window."

"Thank God you're safe," Ivy's mother said, briskly rubbing on the blanket that she'd draped around his stocky form. "Come closer by the fire."

Mrs. Bradford hugged Amy, and her father put a hand on her shoulder.

"Miss Ivy took care of me and helped us put on a play," Amy enthused. "I'm Mary. Will you watch me, Ma?

We can start over."

The woman's grateful gaze met Ivy's. The look in her pale green eyes said what words couldn't. Ivy smiled and nodded in understanding. "I'll just go and get some coffee for everyone."

"I'll come with you." With the quilt wrapped around his shoulders, Craig stood to his feet.

Ivy darted a glance at the others as he walked on ahead of her. Everyone was so wrapped up in their loved ones' return and getting them warm again that Ivy didn't think she or Craig would be missed. Laughter, tears, and thanks filled the parlor, and she silently added her own prayer of gratitude. Strange as it might seem, this Christmas had been one of the best—and most challenging—she'd ever known.

In the kitchen, a cookstove burned, and the coffeepot simmered. Sweet spice scents of cinnamon and cloves lingered in the air, along with the aroma of rich coffee beans.

Craig abruptly turned Ivy's way. She jerked in surprise, her skirts brushing the wall. Her heart began a lilting cadence at the intense look in his eyes.

"Tell me again," he said. "I'm not sure I heard right the first time. Do you plan on staying in Leaning Tree?"

"Yes."

"For good?"

"Yes."

He raised one brow. "Do I dare hope your decision might have something to do with me?"

At least two-thirds of it does. "It might," she said. It was one thing to be remorseful for needlessly slighting him in the past; it was quite another to throw herself at the man.

A slow grin curled his mouth. "I've got enough money saved up to build a house come spring—the kind you like with wooden walls and floors and a roof. If you'd consent to be my wife, Ivy, you'd make me the happiest man in all of Nebraska."

"Craig Watson!" Exasperated, she shook her head, though her heart beat triple time at his words and she couldn't prevent the smile that stretched her cheeks. "Before introducing the subject of marriage, don't you think you should at least ask to court me properly?"

"Would you agree?"

A sudden case of shyness hit. "I might."

"To both?"

"Yes," she whispered.

Craig whooped in delight and cast the quilt from his shoulders. Sliding his large hands about her waist, he twirled her once around the confined space. She squealed when his leg knocked against the table. Dishes clattered, silverware clinked, and she laughingly protested that he put her down before someone came into the room and saw them. He set her gently on her feet, his brown eyes rich with amusement and warmth.

"I'll always love you, my proper Boston girl. I knew it from the first day I saw you stepping off that dusty wagon with your chin a mile high in the air."

Before she could think to be indignant about his teasing remark, Craig dipped his head and tenderly kissed her, and Ivy forgot all else but him.

Adapted from an old prairie cookbook, this recipe is for thin, biscuit-like chocolate-frosted cookies—perfect for a Christmas tea or small party.

3 egg whites
5 tablespoons powdered sugar
2 egg yolks (well beaten)
1/2 teaspoon vanilla
1/2 cup flour
1/4 teaspoon salt
Powdered sugar for coating

Beat egg whites until stiff. Add powdered sugar. In a separate bowl, beat yolks. Fold into mixture. Add vanilla. Fold in flour and salt until batter is well blended. Line a cookie sheet with waxed paper. Press the batter through a pastry bag and onto cookie sheet, forming strips approximately 4 inches long and 1 inch wide. (I use a plastic freezer bag with one tiny section snipped off at a bottom corner for a pastry bag.) Sprinkle with powdered sugar. Bake at 350 degrees for 10 minutes. Edges should be light golden brown. Remove from oven. After a minute, while cookies are still warm, slide spatula underneath to loosen them from waxed paper. Frost or dip in chocolate when cool. Makes approximately 24 cookies.

CHOCOLATE FROSTING/SAUCE:

Stir over low heat 1 cup powdered sugar, ½ cup semi-sweet chocolate chips, and ⅛ cup water until rich and creamy. As it cools, it thickens and makes a sweet frosting to spread over cookies. Or put back on low heat and add several drops more water until thin enough to use as a dipping sauce.

Pamela Griffin lives in North Central Texas and divides her time among God, family, and writing. Her main goal in writing Christian fiction is to encourage others and plant seeds of faith through entertaining stories that minister to the wounded spirit. Christmas is her favorite time of year, and she enjoys writing stories centered on the season. She has contracted over twenty novels and novellas and loves hearing from her readers. You can visit her at: http://users.waymark.net/words_of_honey/.

THE CHRISTMAS NECKLACE

by Maryn Langer

Chapter 1

Chicago—October 8, 1871

A rumble like the sound of an approaching train rolled through Lucinda Porter's dream, growing louder and louder until the roar enveloped her. It continued to roar, not lessening, not moving on. Lucinda rolled onto her back and worried herself awake. *Trains never sound that loud for this long.*

She jerked off her sleeping mask and sat up, puzzled by the crimson light filtering into her canopied bed. She tore open the brocade bed curtain and stared in disbelief through the wall of windows across the room. Flames licked at bare branches of the ancient sycamore. Black smoke seeped in around the window frame.

From outside her room came a rattling, a pounding on the door. "Mistress! Mistress!" The lock gave way and Pearl, nanny of her childhood and now beloved personal maid, rushed in with two serving girls. Lucinda bolted out of bed, grabbed a velvet dressing gown, and struggled into it.

"Hurry, Mistress," Pearl pleaded. Strong hands rammed satin slippers onto Lucinda's feet.

The sycamore exploded into a giant torch of white light. Windows blackened and cracked. Smoke came from everywhere and filled the room. Coughing and with eyes streaming, they stumbled toward the hallway. Blistering heat enveloped the room, and the roar of red-yellow flames swallowed up all other sound.

Terror muted her, muted them all. They gripped hands to make a human chain and rushed, stumbling, choking, into the hallway. Lucinda, Pearl, and the loyal serving maids staggered half seeing down the grand staircase to the foyer. They stepped onto the marble tile and fumbled their way through the smoke across the foyer, down the back passageway, and out the servants' entrance into the cool October evening. Lucinda took her first deep breath and stopped. Pearl wrapped her arm around Lucinda's shoulder and guided her to safety.

Lucinda twisted about in time to see the home of her

childhood, sanctuary in her widowhood, haven after the sudden loss of both parents, and one of the most beautiful houses in Chicago collapse into a great bonfire. She searched for voice to scream her pain but found none. Her lungs burned, her heart hurt, her legs buckled.

Peoria, Illinois—December 22, 1871

A heavy hand shook Lucinda. "Lady, wake up," a weary voice said. "It's mid-morning and train's about to leave Peoria. You ain't got a ticket to go beyond."

Lucinda Porter jerked awake and blinked up into the furrowed, mocha-colored face of the uniformed conductor. "What? Who?" *How dare he speak to me in such a familiar manner.*

"You almost missed your station."

Where is Pearl? I can't miss my station. Why didn't she wake me? Lucinda shook her head to clear the confusion. Slowly, the heartbreaking reality of Pearl's leaving settled in again. She had departed two months ago, but Lucinda still couldn't fully accept that she wasn't there. Forcing the painful memories back into hiding, she sat up and slid forward on the wooden bench. She pulled her ill-fitting, secondhand coat tightly about her and glanced down at serviceable, over-the-ankle brogans. Impoverished and alone, the finality of her situation sent a chill that rattled her bones.

During this past week, she had been reduced financially to a class lower than that of the conductor. She felt ill at ease in his presence, but she forced a tremulous smile. "Thank you for your concern. I must have been exhausted to fall asleep so soundly," she managed to say.

Apprehension registered in his eyes as he waited.

"My experiences of the past two months have left me fatigued." Her words were mumbled, hurried. The conductor raised his eyebrows. "The Great Chicago fire destroyed my home and everything in it."

Why should he care? Their lives would likely never touch again. Daily he would keep his train on schedule, and she, by early afternoon, would become a kitchen maid at the Tillotson mansion outside Peoria. At least there, though she was not of that world any longer, she would be tucked away in familiar circumstances. She could lick her wounds and try to put her life back together.

"Ohhh, I see," the man said. "Mrs. O'Leary's cow what kicked the bucket burned ya out, so you've come to Peoria to spend Christmas with relatives, have you?"

Lucinda gathered her worn carpetbag and stepped into

the aisle. "I have no relatives, here nor anywhere. I've come to Peoria as a domestic at Judge Marshall Tillotson's country estate." *There, you have my pathetic story in one sentence.* Hearing her own words forced her to finally accept the hard truth of her new station in life. She couldn't pretend anymore that this new life was a bad dream and would go away.

"I'm sorry that you have to go out in the storm. It's comin' straight across the prairie. Nary a tree to break the wind." Gently, he held her arm and moved her along the aisle and down the steps to the platform. "This storm's gonna be a real humdinger. You got someone to meet you?"

She looked up and studied his eyes, his face. He knew little about her situation yet seemed genuinely anxious for her welfare. *Amazing. Why should he give me a second thought?* It had never occurred to her that, with the exception of Pearl, her servants and others of the serving class truly cared about her comfort and well-being. This notion needed some more pondering.

"I'm sure my transportation to the Tillotsons' will be along." At her weak smile, the conductor's face relaxed somewhat, and he climbed the steps. Over the clanking and grinding of the train into motion, he shouted, "Have a merry Christmas."

His well-meant words stabbed her heart. This

Christmas would not be merry. No magnificent tree in a foyer that was larger than many homes, no welcoming candles lighting twenty-three sparkling windows. There would be no teas, no balls, no banquets, no Christmas Eve service with her parents in the family pew, no expensive gifts spilling from under a tree whose top star reached the second-story balcony. This Christmas she would not accompany her mother in directing the preparation and delivery of baskets heaped high with food and clothing for the unfortunate.

A year ago she had become a widow before she reached her twenty-first birthday. Last July she was orphaned, and this December she was left completely without means. Even Pearl was living a pampered life with her wealthy sister while Lucinda had become one of those unfortunates.

Shivering in the oversized coat and ugly blue and yellow striped cap, she watched the caboose sway off down the tracks. Not until the train became a distant blur did she remember that her small trunk had not been put off. Except for her sweater and nightgown in the carpetbag, everything she owned was in that trunk.

Her heart lurched, and her hand flew to her chest. Hidden beneath her navy wool dress, the precious antique necklace with flawless emeralds the color of her eyes was still there. It was the first and last Christmas present from her late beloved husband, the seventh earl of Northland. Lucinda pressed her hand against the precious gift and fought back tears, thankful she had fallen asleep wearing it on the night everything burned.

Hopeful, she looked around the platform. Except for the stationmaster in his little box of an office, the station was deserted. Remembering her new class in life, it dawned on her that a servant of such lowly rank wouldn't likely have someone waiting to convey her. Those charged with the transport of common serving maids weren't known to be prompt or polite. Sent on more errands than one, picking up the new kitchen help was probably last on their list before they left for home.

She crossed the street in front of the station and stood where she would be visible to any passing conveyance. The street corner offered no protection from the wind; gust after gust swept over her, biting through her coat. Shivering, she pulled the collar tighter about her throat and moved back into a warehouse doorway, looking up and down the empty street. At last, the smart *clip-clop* of horses' hooves broke the silence.

"Oh, thank you, thank you," Lucinda whispered. A large enclosed sleigh came into view. She rushed into the street where she could more easily be seen. The sleek team drew alongside. The driver gave her nary a glance and raced on, leaving a miniature blizzard behind. Fine snow settled over Lucinda and marked the departure of the only transportation to have traveled that way.

"They aren't coming for me." She wilted against the building, her courage draining. "Maybe they don't expect me. Maybe I don't even have a position." A tear she couldn't contain slid down her cheek and froze. Lucinda found a clean handkerchief and wiped her nose. "Oh, Pearl, I miss you so. You would know what to do." It then occurred to Lucinda that she should have asked the stationmaster for advice before she stepped into this freezing, awful wind.

She limped on numb feet back across the street to the little building and related her situation to the old man. The stationmaster shook his head. "Mistress Tillotson don't furnish transport coming or going. You get out there the best way you can, and it's mighty hard to leave once you're there."

"But I'm expected to arrive by early afternoon, or I shan't have a position. What am I to do?" She blinked back threatening tears.

"Best I can suggest is you go over to Main Street. Maybe you can catch a ride on a farm wagon. They come along that way all the time. With it being the last Friday before Christmas and a storm coming in, if you hurry, you might find one."

Lucinda thanked him. Fighting against a blend of panic and misery at being so helpless, she limped away through the blowing snow toward Main Street.

Chapter 2

D avid Morgan stood in the hall outside the sitting room of Mistress Rosella Tillotson's townhouse and adjusted his cravat. He removed his mouton Cossack hat and ran a hand along the sides of his blue-black hair in a futile attempt to smooth it. Calling on Mrs. Tillotson before noon probably wasn't the wisest thing he had done in his life, but time was running out. The Tillotsons were leaving in two weeks for an extended trip to Paris for the winter season.

I must find the good judge today. Remind the kindly old man to write the referral letter he promised.

He shucked off his overcoat and knocked with a firm rap on the ornately carved door.

"A pox on your generations. It's not yet ten," called a woman's voice, deep and gravelly. "Who's the degenerate cur who can't tell time?"

"David. David Morgan, Mistress Tillotson."

"David?" Her harsh voice changed to beckoning satin. "Since when have you started knocking?"

What is that supposed to mean? I always knock.

"Come in this minute and explain why you've been neglecting me, you naughty boy."

An unremarkable girl in a gray uniform opened the door. David entered the sitting room and handed her his hat and coat.

Though professional decorators had tried to create elegance, Rosella's taste for heavy furniture upholstered with bold textured fabric overpowered the classic objects of art the Tillotsons had collected from around the world.

Rosella fit with the surroundings perfectly. Society matron of Peoria, wife of renowned Judge Marshall Tillotson, she reclined in a regal pose on an elaborately carved chaise lounge. She was robed in a white satin dressing gown and propped amid plump pillows in burgundy satin cases. Mistress Tillotson laid aside a large hand mirror and smiled a coquettish welcome to David. "Come. Sit and tell me what is happening in the outside world." She sat up and patted the foot of the burgundy velvet chaise.

He ignored her command. "I've come hoping the judge was here."

"I suspect he's in the country. We are having a Christmas party this evening, you know." She patted the chaise again.

He deliberately walked to the fireplace. Nodding toward the newly hired maid hovering in the doorway to the bedroom, he asked, "What happened to Gigi?"

"Gigi, that ungrateful wench! She ate her way into a waddling, shiftless mountain of fat. Cost me a fortune to keep her in uniforms. Three days ago, without a second's notice, she up and left. Disappeared. Vanished without a trace." Rosella's eyes, an unusual autumn green with gold flecks, glared at him as though this disaster were his fault.

David shook his head. *The woman is impossible. No wonder Judge Tillotson stays away.*

She picked up the mirror and pursed her lips. "What a pity I don't rouge my lips. I could wipe them clean and add another touch to my invalid's ruse." She looked over the top of the mirror at him, eyes twinkling. "Can you not see, David, how very ill I am?"

He folded his arms. "Why, may I ask, are you playing the invalid?"

"I must look sick enough to convince Marshall that I am unable to attend that wretched dinner he insists on having in the country this evening."

"Why did you agree to have it if you didn't want to attend? I fail to understand the need for the charade. There's a storm predicted for today. And coming in on this *particular* day, you could just say that you don't feel well enough emotionally to cope with such an affair."

Her eyes narrowed. "You remember what day this is?"

"How could I forget? You've reminded me every December 22 for the past five years. But you've never gone to this extreme to celebrate your grief."

Rosella drew back her hand and flung the mirror at the wall. David jumped out of the way of scattering shards that fell like ice crystals onto the oriental carpet. "Mistress Tillotson, throwing things is going too far."

She didn't acknowledge his scolding. "I wonder why Marshall doesn't remember? Meghan was his daughter, too. The fact is, the way he doted on her sickened me."

"Of course he remembers, but he needs friends to help him through the pain."

Rosella's expression softened. "Meghan would have been twenty-two today." Her voice trembled. "She's been gone twenty years—a lifetime." Rosella reached for her linen handkerchief and blotted the tear threatening to streak her powder. "To this day, I cannot believe someone could creep into the house and snatch a sleeping child from her crib without leaving a trace. Not a clue could the

Pinkerton detectives find. Two years of searching and they never found how she left Peoria." Rosella buried her face in the handkerchief.

David watched the performance and felt a churning start in the pit of his stomach.

Rosella dabbed around her eyes and snapped her fingers. "Girl, get me another mirror."

The maid quickly handed a replacement to Rosella, who ignored David and checked her makeup for damage. David pulled out his pocket watch. The morning was slipping away. "I must—"

"I'm really glad you dropped by this morning. I'd like for us to have a little visit before lunch." Rosella stood and walked slowly toward him.

He edged away from the fireplace. "What do you want to visit about?"

"Your going to Paris."

"Paris! I don't want to go anywhere close to Paris," he said bluntly. "What I want is to go west, not east."

She shuddered. "West? Have you lost your senses? The West is unfinished. Nothing but sagebrush, Indians, and other wild things."

"The far West is new territory. A man can get a foothold. Become anything he wants to."

"That's nonsense. What is it you want to become that

you can't achieve right here in Peoria? After we get back from Paris."

He was amazed at how innocent her smile appeared, how convincing her eyes. "Before *you* get back, I shall be gone."

Rosella's mouth took a cunning twist into a half-smile that he had learned spelled danger.

"David," she said ever so sweetly, "I've given the past five years to turning you, a raw Welsh immigrant, into a gentleman with the savoir faire to be my escort in Paris. And I just spent a king's ransom on my wardrobe and yours."

"Rosella, you've been telling everyone you and the judge are going."

She wasn't listening. *She's already plotting her revenge.*

Her thin smile sent a shiver down his spine. "That is no way to repay the kindness I have extended you. That makes me very unhappy. And Marshall won't be happy, either."

"That sounds like a threat, Rosella. I repeat, you've told—"

"About a month ago, Marshall decided he couldn't go. Too many court cases on the docket, or so he says. So, David dear, because I am going and I will not go without an escort, you *are* going."

"No, Rosella, I'm not." He turned to the maid. "Please bring me my coat."

Fury darkened Rosella's face. "Hear me well, my young friend." Her eyes sparked a look he had seen turned on others. Never on him.

Her hand shot out, lightning fast, and grabbed his wrist. Rosella stared hard into his face. "If you think you can run away on a whim, think again. If you even consider such a thing, I shall tell Marshall you took advantage of my disturbed state during this upsetting time of the year—Meghan's disappearance—and you forced yourself on me."

"You would be lying and would have to prove those accusations in court, Mistress Tillotson." David clamped his jaw tight, revealing none of his own rage.

"Ha! Don't you worry about court. Have you any idea what Marshall would do to you? You'd be ruined!" Her evil smile suddenly turned sweet. "But enough of this. Look over there, dear." She waited until he looked. "See the lists on my desk? I have a million things to attend to."

He started to speak, but she cut him off with a wave of her hand.

Her mood shifted, and her voice was now light and happy as a child's. "Your wardrobe is ready at the tailor's. Pick it up, and I'll send word so you can accompany me to the country."

David grabbed his hat and coat from the maid and left without a word. He stormed down the stairs, jamming his hat on his head and his arms into his coat as he went. Propelled by fury, he scarcely noticed the storm or the stately homes he passed as he stalked toward Peoria's downtown and his boardinghouse across the tracks.

Rounding the corner of Jefferson and Main, he came face to face with an ill-dressed waif. They collided, and she went spinning toward the street. He grabbed for her, managing to get a grip on her coat, stopping her fall. Angry and frustrated, David forgot both when he looked down into her eyes—clear green with flecks of gold, framed by long, smoky lashes. Her eyes. . .they reminded him of someone.

Little else of her face showed between the striped woolen cap pulled down to just above her eyes and the large coat collar covering her cheeks. But the eyes: He couldn't help staring. They held him captive, nearly drowning him in the sorrow reflected there. Only once before had he seen such deep sadness. When his father was killed in the coal mines of Wales, his mother's eyes never lost that look. *What has happened to you, little mud lark, to scar you so?*

He let go of her coat and stepped back. "I'm so sorry. Are you hurt?" She shook her head, and an auburn curl escaped from her cap. Her coat was soaked, and snow spilled over her shoe tops. "You are not properly dressed for such weather. You must get inside at once."

"Indeed, I shall avail myself at the first opportunity."

He smiled. She might look like a poor waif, but her speech was that of a lady. Interesting. He wondered what she looked like without that unsightly cap. He gestured at the three-story brick structure across the street. "The Pinkney Building is a good place to get warm. The bakery there is the best in town."

She thanked him, and he watched as she slipped and slid her away across the street. The bakery would be warm. They would give her a free sample of the day's special. Once in front of the three-story building where Judge Tillotson had his offices, she looked back at him, nodded, then disappeared inside.

Alone on the empty street, David's frustration returned. With every step, he seethed at Rosella's cunning entrapment. Indeed he had escorted her through five years of social events, but it was at the insistence of her husband who never seemed to be available. *Now I know why. She's demented,* he thought.

By the time David reached his room at the boardinghouse, he could see no way to gracefully disentangle himself except to flee far and fast. He knelt before the steamer trunk given to him by his mother. Taking out the little coffer locked away inside, he counted the money he had saved. Eighty-four dollars, after the payment of his room and board. Enough to take him west if he guarded his spending.

He decided to accept the suit Rosella promised him. The tailor shop was in his neighborhood, so he hurried over. There, to his chagrin, he found a complete wardrobe waiting. A month ago when he went in to be fitted for one suit, he had no idea what Rosella had planned. It took two trips for David to carry his new wardrobe to his room.

From the mountain of items laid neatly on his bed, he chose the tuxedo for the dinner at the Tillotsons' prairie mansion. His mind raced as he carefully folded the items of clothing into his soft-sided leather case. "I know one thing. I am not going to the country with Rosella. Or anywhere else."

David snapped the case shut and changed into his riding clothes. "I shall stop over at the judge's office and write the referral letter. Then all he'll have to do is sign it, and I'll be out of Rosella's clutches before tomorrow dawns."

Chapter 3

Inside the spice-scented bakery, Lucinda sat thawing her nearly frozen extremities and sampling immodest amounts of oatmeal cookies, lemon custard pie, and cherry cobbler the owners urged on her. Business was brisk, but in the dim corner where she was seated on a crate near the ovens, no one paid her any mind. While she ate, she took stock of her situation.

For the first time, she allowed herself to review the events of last Wednesday. Was it only two days ago that she had still thought of herself as the wealthy Countess Lucinda Porter, fresh out of widow's weeds? Though her house and buildings had burned to the ground, she did own the ground. Her father's business partner, whom she called Uncle, took care of the legalities. After the fire, she had stayed in his lavish home and been treated with great kindness but not allowed to look at the books. Wednesday last, he had sat her down and told her the whole story.

Papa always assured Lucinda and Mama that they would always be well cared for. Never did anyone dream he would be temporarily deep in debt and both parents would die in a carriage accident before the debts could be paid. Uncle tried everything he knew to save her estate, he said. But even with the infusion of her inheritance, there was only enough money to pay off half the loans. However, he assured her he would gladly assume her debt if she would marry him. Uncle was a man twice her age, pompous and demanding. She quickly understood she would become his hostage until the debt was paid. She signed over her property to him.

Having chosen poverty, here she was in Peoria.

Lucinda's reverie was interrupted when a tall, thin woman dressed in calico and moccasins walked into the bakery from the interior darkness of the back hallway. Long dark hair pulled into double braids down her back framed her furrowed bronze face. Taking no notice of Lucinda, the woman began checking the contents of the ovens. When she finished, she straightened up and walked over to Lucinda.

Lucinda blushed at having been caught in her silent examination. Clear, nearly colorless blue eyes stared at her with an intensity that felt to Lucinda like they pierced her soul. She felt a deep connection to the old woman and, with it, a tremor of anticipation.

"I am known to all as Yarrow Woman. You are a stranger here." Her voice enfolded Lucinda like a warm blanket. She hadn't felt this safe since before the fire.

"Yes. I'm seeking transportation to the Tillotson estate. I'm expected this afternoon to assume duties as a kitchen maid."

The old woman looked deep into Lucinda's eyes. "I have been prayerfully searching for some answers about my future, and I now have the feeling you and I are going to be bound together somehow." Taking Lucinda's hands, she examined them. "You have never served."

Lucinda looked and saw what Yarrow Woman saw— hands soft and manicured. She shook her head.

Yarrow Woman let go of Lucinda's hands and continued to study her. "You will serve the Tillotsons scarcely any time at all and then never anybody else." Her words were soft, her tone reassuring.

Lucinda felt the blood drain from her face. *I cannot fail in my first position. Where will I turn?*

Yarrow Woman's expression softened. "I apologize for upsetting you, but God moves in unexplained ways, and on occasion I receive impressions about a person's future.

I give all praise to the Lord and take no credit unto myself." She waved a work-hardened hand in a gesture of helplessness. "I am not usually this forthright, but I could not seem to contain this message."

Lucinda's heart skipped a beat.

The woman stood quietly, her eyes fixed on Lucinda. "I have never been to such a place, but I see beyond great mountains of granite, across a desert of death, to a city built by silver."

Lucinda shivered and closed her eyes.

"Do not let your necklace be seen. Keep it hidden and in your possession at all cost."

Lucinda's eyes flew open. She felt for the outline under her dress. "Ho—how do you know these things?" she stammered.

"From childhood I have been gifted with second sight. It is not a thing I control. In the Sioux tribe, I was a wise woman. Now that I know Jesus as my Savior, I receive only that which He chooses to give me." She turned and started back toward the shadows.

Lucinda jumped up. "Do you see when I shall go to that far-off land?"

"You will begin the journey tonight, of course." The words were spoken matter-of-factly as she entered the dim hallway.

"Surely not tonight. How will that happen?" Lucinda called, but Yarrow Woman continued down the hallway.

Lucinda felt warmth deep in her chest, yet at the same time she shivered at Yarrow Woman's words. To consider that she could be out of work by tomorrow was frightening. She had no place else to go. Her fingers trembled as she dusted crumbs off her clothes. She wouldn't consider the possibility of being let go. *I must work hard to please and make myself so useful that they will find me irreplaceable.* She thanked the bakery owners and let herself out, vowing to waylay any conveyance that might be moving upon the prairie toward the Tillotson mansion.

Lucinda walked along Main Street's crowded sidewalk, clutching her valise in one ungloved hand and the collar of her coat tightly about her throat with the other. She mulled over her experience in the bakery and decided that people of the working class were kind and honest. She liked them. Surely one of them would give her a ride.

She approached several kind-looking shoppers, but they gave her sharp looks and continued on their way. Desperation drove her to walk in the street, where she hailed sleighs, carts, wagons, any conveyance moving and some that were parked, but all she received were blank stares or curses for her trouble.

The wind picked up, building the drifts ever deeper

until the shoppers gave up and vanished, leaving the streets deserted. "Oh, please, dear Jesus, help me find a ride. Please."

Before the noon church bells chimed, the storm retreated inside low-slung gray clouds. Still, she trudged up and down Main Street, around and through the drifts, battling mounting despair. She kicked at a drift of snow blocking the sidewalk. The more discouraged Lucinda became, the more she clung to Yarrow Woman's words. *She said I would serve scarcely any time at all. But she did say I would serve. That must mean I will get to the Tillotson mansion somehow.*

She walked into the middle of the street and looked both ways but saw no wagons. Not even a rider. What was she to do? She turned her back to the wind and began to cry, no longer able to hide her despair. It was then she heard hoofbeats pounding hard and fast. Before she could move from the center of the street, he was upon her.

He reined the charging horse to a skidding stop. "Excuse me," a deep voice said, "are you or are you not going to cross the street?"

She whirled around and found herself staring up into the face of the fine-looking man who earlier that morning had directed her to the bakery. Now he sat astride a magnificent chestnut stallion that refused to stand still.

With eyebrows knit together, he asked, "Why are you still out in this weather?"

"Ahh. . .my. . .the train left with my trunk on it. I only have what is in that carpetbag." She gestured at the shabby bag resting on the curb. "And I must. . .I am trying to. . ." *Lucinda, you're babbling.* She took a deep breath. "I have the promise of work as a domestic at the Tillotson estate, but I can find no transportation to take me there."

She said a silent prayer of thanks that her voice sounded strong and clear. "I must be there by early afternoon if I'm to claim the position." She kept her unwavering gaze on his face. His skin was a weathered brown common for farmworkers and did not match the gentleman his riding habit and coat suggested. His eyes focused on her with a force that made her uncomfortably aware of how common she must look. Covered with a dusting of snow, peering out from under a boyish woolen cap, the rest of her buried inside the giant coat, she must look awful.

Swallowing hard, she continued to stare at him. His broad shoulders were covered in a stylish long coat layered with a cape buttoned high around his throat. He had a regal tilt to his head, accented by a Cossack hat that gave him the appearance of an English nobleman, a scowling English nobleman. Then he flashed a wide smile that lit his face.

Even in her misery, Lucinda smiled back. Was he as kind as he looked? Had her prayer for a ride been answered? "I would pay you to take me to the estate." Her voice filled with hope, and she opened her palm to show twenty-five cents. "I know this isn't much, but perhaps we could work out an arrangement where I might pay you later. . . ."

His laugh cut her off. "You're not familiar with money, are you?"

She shook her head. "I was served by a woman who took care of all the details of my life."

"You have offered far too much." The horse tossed his head and gave an impatient stamp. "Kambur says it is time we were off. My name is David Morgan, and you are. . . ?"

"Lucinda. Mrs. Lucinda Porter, late of Chicago."

He nodded at the introduction. "You are fortunate, Mrs. Porter. I'm traveling to the Tillotson estate. Put your money away. I shall be happy to deliver you to your destination if you have no objection to riding astride and double."

Dumb with gratitude, she shook her head and picked up her carpetbag. He removed his foot from the stirrup and reached out his hand. "Let me have your satchel." She handed it up to him, and he hung it from the saddle horn opposite his own fine case. She hiked up her skirt, slid her square-toed brogan into the empty stirrup, and let herself be pulled up behind him. Ladies generally rode sidesaddle, but she wasn't going to point that out.

"Put your arms around my waist and hang on," he ordered. "I don't relish being out in this weather longer than necessary."

Gingerly, she reached around his waist.

"My dear lady, this is no time to be shy. I mean to ride hard, and if I cannot feel your arms, you'll probably land in the road at the first corner. Now slide closer so your face rests against my back, and lock your hands together in front." His brusque voice left no room for argument.

Lest she be left behind, Lucinda positioned herself tight against his back and clasped her hands around his waist. Even from the back, this man radiated power, someone to be reckoned with.

"That's better," he said and flicked the reins. The horse leaped forward. They whirled away up the steep incline and out onto the prairie.

As they flew along, she silently repeated his name, David Morgan, an important name she must not forget. When she was sure she would not forget his name, she began to wonder just how much twenty-five cents was. It must be a goodly sum. She must learn about money.

All she had to her name was contained in the small trunk left on the train and the well-used carpetbag—and of course, her necklace and the clothes on her back. She reminded herself that she was probably going to be known as Lucy Porter, household servant, hoping to arrive at the Tillotson estate in time to serve other people's lavish Christmas parties.

She sighed and let her thoughts drift to this man she was clinging to. She was certain that the likes of David Morgan would not normally give the current version of Lucinda Porter a second glance. That he did said much about him. But such a man was bound to have a beautiful lady waiting at the Tillotsons', most likely his wife. *If he isn't married, Lucinda, he's far above your station now.*

The sky lightened the farther into the country they rode. Lucinda studied the beautiful homes on expansive grounds. A majestic red brick house, clearly visible at the top of a rise, caught her fancy. It cheered her when they turned up the wide road that led toward the front entrance guarded by thick white columns—the Tillotson mansion. However, they veered to the left onto the tradesmen's narrow lane that ran alongside the house. She had never entered a house through the servants' entrance. Once more she was reminded of who she had become.

A hedge of tall yew, pruned to unnatural perfection, screened the lower windows of the house. At the back, the lane widened into a cobblestone yard that separated the kitchen wing from the carriage house and stables. David stopped at the kitchen door. Lucinda held still as he swung his leg over Kambur's neck and landed on the ground at her feet. He offered up his hand. She took it, and their gazes locked for a moment. Quickly, she came to her senses and concentrated on getting off the horse with some degree of grace.

David carried her satchel and ushered her up the steps. "With the dinner hour drawing near, there's such chaos in the kitchen that a cannon blast would go unnoticed. They'll never hear you knock." Handing her the carpetbag, he pounded on the door with no success. He shrugged and said, "Just go on in."

He looked intently into her eyes. "I hate to leave you like this, but three days ago, the good Andy Henderson, head groomsman, and his wife left in the middle of the night. I'm sure the stables are in a muddle since most of the guests are already here. I owe it to the judge to set things straight." He gave her hand a slight squeeze and, with easy grace, swung onto Kambur.

"Thank you," she called and waved. David returned her wave before he rode on to the stables.

He didn't really squeeze my hand, did he? You're imagining things. A combination of emotions raced inside—unexpected attraction to Mr. Morgan and pure terror of facing an unfamiliar kitchen from the servant's side of the fanning doors.

Cautiously, Lucinda tried the latch. It lifted, and the heavy door swung open on silent hinges. A rush of hot air filled with a mix of savory aromas swept over her as she stepped inside.

Chapter 4

How she wished for Mr. Morgan's comforting presence as she stepped into an unfamiliar kitchen for a job she had never done. She stared in disbelief at the sea of humanity running in all directions. To keep from getting trampled, she huddled in the corner and surveyed the kitchen. At the far end of the room and up seven stone steps were the fanning doors that separated the main house from the kitchen and service pantry. Serving maids wearing toadstool-shaped hats bustled in and out through the doors, carrying linens, trays of flatware, and condiments.

They would be bringing in empty plates and carrying out the next course if the meal had begun. Relief surged through her; she had made it in time. Very soon she would be one of those servants, indistinguishable from the others unless someone looked closely. No one probably would unless she did something inappropriate.

Lucinda had never studied formal dinner preparations in the detail she did now, but she knew these girls would keep their harried pace until long after the dinner hour. Guilt sprang up when she remembered her uncaring attitude in the past toward those who served her. Especially Pearl. *I was so ungrateful. I took her for granted. Now she's gone, and I have to fend for myself. I deserve this fate. I truly do.*

The kitchen was almost as large as the one in her English manor house, and the floor and the walls were tiled bright red. Against the outside wall stood a copper sink with water piped directly into it. The Tillotsons must truly be rich to afford such a luxury. Young servant girls stood on stools before the sink, elbow-deep in dishwater, scrubbing endless stacks of pots and pans. From the wood range, Lucinda caught the aromas of burning fruitwood and tantalizing spices. It had been many hours since she had eaten, and her mouth watered.

The kitchen was sweltering. The large cook, autocratic ruler of her domain, mopped the sweat from her face with a Turkish towel round her neck. She was in the process of hoisting a huge baron of beef from the oven onto the chopping block in the middle of the room.

She looked up from testing the roast and spotted Lucinda. She pointed at one of the maids. "You, Molly! Come." Molly came running down the stairs. "See who's hiding in the shadows by the door. If it's a dirty tramp begging food, lay this frying pan across his back." She grabbed up a heavy black skillet and thrust it into Molly's small hands.

Lucinda hadn't thought of herself as looking like a tramp, and she wasn't going to cower in the corner. She moved out of the shadows and watched Molly cross the kitchen.

At a safe distance, she stopped. "Mrs. Kidd, do I. . ."

"Get on with it, girl."

"Yes, Mrs. Kidd." Molly straightened to her full five feet and raised the pan over her head. "Get out, you ruffian! Get out afore I split yer skull." Her voice squeaked like an adolescent boy's and made a mockery of the threat.

Clutching her satchel, Lucinda pushed back her cap and began walking toward Molly, never taking her eyes from the skillet. *If I don't assert myself right now, I'll become the goat for the entire staff.* She brushed by Molly and said in a firm voice, "I am the new maid Mr. Button engaged. Please let him know I have arrived."

Not used to such boldness, the other servants stopped in their tracks and gawked at Lucinda. *Good. They shall not know how frightened I am. Let them think I'm a trusted colleague of the mighty Mr. Button.* From managing her own house, she knew that the butler was the person to watch out for. He ran the staff upstairs and was absolute dictator below.

Mrs. Kidd was first to recover her composure. "Well, goose, go fetch him," she thundered.

Still clutching the frying pan, Molly fled past Lucinda, up the stairs, and through one fanning door as Mr. Button entered the kitchen through the other. His cherubic face remained calm, but round eyes, partially obscured by bushy black brows, narrowed as he drew closer to Lucinda. "Ah, you are Mrs. Porter?" he asked in an adenoidal voice.

The effect of the imperious Mr. Button bearing down on Lucinda caused her to stand tall and tip up her chin. Then she remembered her position and lowered her eyes as became a domestic servant.

"So you have deigned to finally honor us with your presence. Early afternoon, as you promised, would have been much preferable. However, we're a bit short of help, so I won't throw you out with the chickens just yet."

They needed her, so she could afford to establish herself a bit higher in the pecking order. "Circumstances prevented an earlier arrival." She spoke firmly.

"I see," said Mr. Button. "I understand your experience is limited."

"I have had no experience in this country. In England, however, I spent two years with the earl of Northland." She stopped short of mentioning that she spent it as his wife. "I worked with the staff of a very large manor house. I am capable of serving in any area where I am required."

He cast a jaundiced eye over her from head to foot.

Lucinda knew her worn coat and cap certainly did nothing to validate her claims. "All I had in this world was destroyed in the great Chicago fire last October. I have been forced to accept the generosity of others for my needs."

He sniffed and nodded. "Are you sensible and literate as your papers say?" His left nostril twitched in time to his words.

"The papers are correct," she said, giving an autocratic lift to her words. "I am both sensible and literate. Trained by the royals of England, I remain today on the most intimate terms with Lady North."

"Yes, yes, you come highly recommended. Have you brought sufficient aprons in good repair for housework? And suitable apparel for your afternoon off, if you are found worthy to be granted one?"

"I did. However, my trunk was not put off the train."

"Late and no aprons. Not an auspicious beginning. What are you called?" he asked sharply.

"My name is Lucinda. Lucinda Porter, sir," she said over the steady chug of the water pump in the background. When she pulled off her cap, auburn curls tumbled over her shoulders. She lowered the collar away from her face and bobbed a curtsy.

His eyes widened and his left nostril twitched violently. "Yes, well. . ." He cleared his throat. "A bit pretentious, I'd say. Lucy seems more appropriate."

Lucinda debated with herself but a moment. "Perhaps Lucy is more appropriate for a serving girl, sir, but Lucinda is my name, and I prefer it."

Mr. Button smiled. "A girl with spirit has a place. However, I hope, Lucy, you know the time and place."

He turned toward Mrs. Kidd. "Though the mistress has not yet arrived, Judge Tillotson says we are to serve dinner. And you, Lucy. . ."

Lucinda winced at the name but held herself in the best servant stance. "Yes, sir?"

"You will be assigned a post in the dining room. We shall assess the quality of your work while you serve dinner. Molly, take Lucy into the press for a fresh white apron and cap and show her how they are to be worn."

Lucinda followed Molly down a dim hallway and into the laundry press. Her back to the entrance, a lone woman stoked wood into the small, cast-iron range. Half a dozen irons of different sizes heated on the top of the stove, and a wrinkled sheet lay on the ironing board to press. Molly walked over and placed her arm around the woman's shoulder. "I've brought the new girl in for an apron and hat."

The woman straightened and gave Molly a tired smile. "You know where they're kept. Help yourself." Molly scurried away. The frail woman wiped her hands on a towel and returned to the ironing board with a fresh iron.

Lucinda studied the piles of laundry neatly arranged by color near the washtubs. *I hope I never have to work here. This has to be the hottest, hardest work in any house.* "Do you do all this work alone?" she asked.

The woman looked up. Her face paled. "Oh, my," she gasped and rushed to shut the door into the linen keep.

"Pearl?" Lucinda cried out in disbelief, and they flew into each other's arms. "Oh, Pearl, I can't believe it's you. What are you doing here? You told me you were going to live with your rich sister."

"Lucinda?" Pearl stepped back; her expression looked as though she would faint. "Is Molly getting the uniform for *you*?"

Lucinda touched Pearl's cheek. "Why are *you* here in the laundry press? Where is the rich sister who needed you to come be with her?"

"I am living in my rich sister's house. But no matter. I want to hear about you, my dearest child. Why are you here?" Pearl studied Lucinda. "You look. . ." Her eyes filled with tears. "What has happened to you?"

All that Lucinda had bottled up came out in a tumble of words. "Wednesday last, Uncle announced it was his unpleasant duty to tell me that I was no longer wealthy. In fact, I was deeply in debt. Papa had unfortunate financial reverses, so he took on many loans. When Mama and Papa were killed, all that indebtedness fell on Uncle's shoulders. He said he must repay these huge loans or the business was doomed. And there was no hope of rebuilding my home. Uncle assured me that my only option was to declare bankruptcy."

"But what happened to your settlement from Lord North's estate?" Pearl asked. "That was substantial."

"It all went to pay off loans, according to Uncle."

Pearl's brow creased. "But if it was your money that cleared the loans, shouldn't you own the land?"

"I did own it, but there's no money to pay off the other loans. Uncle handed me sheaf after sheaf of papers. After I scanned them, I signed away everything."

Pearls eyes widened. "Not your necklace." She spoke in a whisper.

Lucinda shook her head and put hand over her heart. "Uncle finally let me keep it." She glanced anxiously at the door into the linen keep, certain that Molly would be returning soon. "He said he had to sell his house and all he could scrape together to put against the debt or the business would fail. He had no money and suggested that I visit an intelligence service to find work as a domestic. So here I am."

Pearl wrapped Lucinda in her arms and crooned, "Your papa was a fine businessman, but I knew there had been financial reversals. I had no idea they were so severe. Only a few days before. . .the Fourth of July, I heard him tell your mama he had made an exceptional sale that would clear all their debt and permanently assure their financial future. Oh, my poor girl." She released Lucinda. "Hurry, tell the rest."

"I must have looked stricken, because Uncle offered me money to tide me over until I could locate work. I thanked him and told him that I would get on just fine."

Pearl caressed Lucinda's cheek. "So you went to the intelligence office and found work with the Tillotsons. But how did you get from the train station to here?"

"Mr. David Morgan was kind enough to bring me."

The mere mention of his name made her glow inside.

Pearl nodded. "A fine young man." She held Lucinda at arm's length. "Is the mistress home?"

"I don't think so. I overheard it said that we are to serve dinner without her."

"Then some quick words, my dear. Listen carefully. Stay out of sight as much as possible. Never turn your back on your betters, and never meet their eyes. Speak clearly but only as much as is necessary."

"Thank you, Pearl. I will be respectful in all ways, but I don't plan to spend the rest of my life as a domestic—"

Molly threw open the door and bustled into the press. "Land, Pearl, you had the aprons on the top shelf, and I liked never to have found one her size. Come, Lucy, take off that coat and I'll help you with the apron. Thank goodness you have a decent dress on." Molly worked as fast as she talked, helping Lucinda don the apron and hat. "Now you look like a proper servant. Step lively, now. We're to be in the serving pantry."

Pearl glanced toward Molly. "I need a moment with Lucin. . .Lucy. She'll be right out."

Molly shrugged a shoulder and hurried down the hall.

Pearl tucked a copper curl inside Lucinda's mushroom-shaped hat. "For your own sake, keep your head down, your hair covered, and remain in the background. If the mistress arrives, stay as far from her as you decently can. Now hurry off. You'll do just fine."

Reluctantly, Lucinda left the comfort of Pearl's company. Fighting back tears, she walked slowly down the hallway, mindful of each step that took her farther from her predictable past into an unpredictable future.

"Lucinda? We seem to have a tendency to run into each other," a deep velvet voice said.

She turned quickly, her gloom lifting. "Mr. Morgan? Whatever are you doing in the servants' wing?"

"I needed to see if you were all right. I dumped you off like a sack of potatoes and left you to fend for yourself. I've felt guilty ever since. The least I can do is apologize for not seeing you safely inside."

With a faint smile, she asked, "What exactly is your position here, Mr. Morgan?"

He laughed. "You are a courageous little one, aren't you?"

"Are you avoiding my question?"

"On the contrary, I was buying time while I tried to determine what exactly my position is. First of all, please call me David. I am uncomfortable with being Mr. Morgan to you."

That wouldn't be difficult since she had been thinking of him as David all evening. "David it is. And I'm

Lucinda, even though Mr. Button has christened me Lucy. He feels Lucinda is an uppity name."

David laughed again. "Yes, Button, as he is called on this side of the fanning doors, would consider that a threat to his dominion."

"Your position, David?" she reminded. She was desperate to know more about him. Even in the short time she had known him, she had become acutely aware that he was a mighty man. It showed in the way he moved, quick and powerful as the horse he rode. It showed in his eyes, bright and respectful—a rich navy blue she could see now in the light of the corridor. He seemed to know what she was thinking even when she did not speak her thoughts. It showed in his voice, deep, full, to match his speech. He was not given to needless words or courtly phrases but came to the point of things. Yes, she very much wanted to know more about this man.

"Well," he began with some hesitation, "during the past five years I've been a law clerk in Judge Tillotson's office, read for the law with him, escorted Mistress Tillotson to various social events when requested to do so, and shoveled out the stables when the need arose." He pursed his lips. "That pretty much sums up my position."

"You will be a lawyer one day?"

"I think that day may be upon me very soon."

Lucinda's heart sank. "Does that mean you'll be leaving?"

He studied her as though reading her story. "Yes, right away. But now it won't be by choice, and I shall regret having to go."

"You will?"

"I will. Very much."

Molly's worried face appeared behind David. "Lucy, please come. You're going to be in terrible trouble if Mr. Button comes back and you're not in the serving pantry."

David took her hand. "I know this is unacceptably sudden, but I can't bear to think of leaving you just when I've found you. Perhaps later this evening when you have finished your duties. . ." He paused and looked deep into her eyes. "Could we talk? I feel I must know more about you."

"Lucy! Come!" Molly was running toward them.

"Yes, David. You will find me?"

"I will find you."

Molly grabbed Lucinda's arm and guided her away. She looked back before she was propelled through the fanning doors. David stood in the middle of the hall, his eyes focused on her.

Chapter 5

David arrived outside the drawing room as Button was ushering the men from the library into the Tillotsons' elegantly appointed drawing room. The ladies, resplendent in low-cut evening dresses, greeted them. David slipped inside and mingled with the assemblage. The men brought with them the fragrance of bay rum and the pungent scent of smoke from the thick cigars and cheroots that most in the library had smoked. Mixed with the women's heady perfumes from Paris, the aroma was unusual but pleasant.

Then, as was his habit, David retreated to an inconspicuous corner to observe. Though the women wore different colors and fabrics, all wore long skirts drawn back, bunched into an elaborate arrangement at the hip and, over a supporting bustle, draped into a train that swept the floor. No doubt the latest Paris fashion. He imagined Lucinda in such a gown.

He jerked himself up short. He must keep his wits about him if he was to get the judge's signature tonight. He forced himself to stay in the present by studying the gentlemen's attire. They wore flowery waistcoats, impeccably tailored. Most were embellished with watch chains from which jeweled charms dangled. Precious stones anchored wide, colorful cravats. Black or dark blue swallowtail tuxedo jackets, the rage this winter, hung over fawn-colored pantaloons. He couldn't help but notice that in most cases they stretched across ample stomachs.

David ran his hands over his own black frock coat. Thanks to Rosella's excellent tailor, it fit perfectly. He imagined Lucinda next to him, promenading gracefully across the room. A waltz played in his head, and he could feel her in his arms as they pirouetted around the floor. He became so lost in his fantasy he almost missed Judge Tillotson motioning him to join a small group of community leaders.

The judge was short and ruddy of complexion. He had one badly squinting eye, which he habitually kept closed, and his head was oversized for his body. His thick white hair was his best feature. Tonight its sheen glowed in the lamplight like a halo. On the judge, however, the halo effect missed being regal because he had been forced since birth to hold his head stiffly inclined toward his left shoulder. His detractors said his head was askew like a cow with horn-ail. David, on the other hand, thought that Judge Tillotson had a fine presence, giving the impression of a successful and happy man. That is, until one caught him off guard and looked deep into his eyes. Behind the judge's pleasant, summer blue eyes lurked a chained darkness writhing to break free. David had only looked there once.

He came to stand with the group. "Good evening, Judge Tillotson," he said and nodded to the other gentlemen.

"Glad you could join us, my lad. I want the boys to meet a first-rate new lawyer. You'll be hearing of this young man, gentlemen."

David could feel heat rise above his cravat to his cheeks. He clasped his hands behind his back and squared his stance, ready to listen to the judge's current monologue.

Instead, the judge said, "Please excuse us, gentlemen. Business never takes a holiday." He put his strong hand around David's back and guided him to the side of the room. "David, I must admit, I've never worked with a lad that I've enjoyed as much as you." He took a long swallow from his glass of sherry. The judge usually drank nothing stronger than watered wine. Was this his attempt to ease the pain of this day?

The judge continued. "You know that I've come to care about you. Your quick wit and diligence have touched a chord in me. You're a young man with a future."

David flushed again, realizing that praise was harder to handle gracefully than criticism. "Thank you, sir."

"I'm sad to think you'll be moving on soon."

His words caught David off guard. He started to protest, but the judge held up his hand. "Nothing to be ashamed of, son. Be ashamed if you didn't want to strike out for yourself. Besides, you're ready. Where is it you're thinking of going?"

"Well, sir, I do have an article about the possibilities." He pulled a newspaper clipping from his tuxedo pocket, but before he could unfold it, the dinner gong sounded. The judge glanced around the room and then gave David a pat on the back. "I don't believe Mistress Tillotson has arrived yet, but we will be dining without her. Excuse me, David, perhaps we can talk later. Right now I must claim my dinner partner."

"Of course." David mumbled something about finding his own partner. Without Mistress Tillotson, the table would be short one lady. This was not the first time he had waited at the back of the line, ready to escort a neighbor hastily invited.

The double doors to the dining room swung open. Under the scrutiny of the well-organized Mr. Button, the judge and his lady led the guests in to dinner. The table, set for twenty, created a forest of French crystal and English bone china. Holly and evergreen cascaded down from a regiment of tall silver cones spaced along the center. Kerosene lamps on the sideboard, along with rows of candles down the center of the table, gave off a romantic glow. A pair of footmen hired for the occasion stood at attention at the head and foot of the table.

David's dinner partner had a difficult name he never seemed able to recall, a great many large teeth, not to mention arthritic fingers that occasionally gripped his arm or twisted a long rope of pearls. David braced himself for an evening of her nonstop conversation. She immediately launched into the intimate details of how she came to be unmarried.

The woman seated on the other side of David managed to engage him in conversation. But each time David's dinner companion sensed the slightest break, she skillfully turned his attention back to her story, beginning precisely where she had been interrupted. She did not require answers, making it possible for him to contemplate Lucinda. She had the most unusual eyes and a square chin with a delicate cleft. She was captivating yet with a disturbing resemblance to Rosella Tillotson as she must have looked in her early years. That connection gave rise to all manner of speculation.

Thinking about Lucinda was not wise. She so completely took over his concentration that David lost track of the table conversation. He must keep an eye on the judge and anticipate when he would be approachable to sign the referral letter.

To occupy his thoughts, David tried to plan the best route across the prairie in the morning. He tried to think what to take with him. He tried to envision all the things he had to do. He tried, and all he saw was Lucinda's face, Lucinda's smile, and the sadness in her eyes. He could easily drown in the emerald depths of those eyes. He longed to let his fingers trace her delicate forehead and high curving cheekbones, the straight nose, and her full mouth. His hands flexed with the urge to feel her chin with its intriguing cleft and the smooth line of her throat. *Is she the woman for me?* He thought about the circumstances of their meeting. *Is there a divine plan behind this day?*

He scolded himself. This was not the time to be thinking such things.

Just at that moment, across the room from David, a

door opened noiselessly. Half-hidden by a carved wooden screen, a maid emerged wearing one of those absurd English caps. She delivered a large silver tray into Button's hands. He in turn passed the tray to the footman to begin serving.

David forgot all else when he recognized the maid. It was only a glimpse before Lucinda vanished behind the screen, but he knew well that intense, pale face with a copper-bright lock of hair escaping from the cap. His heart leaped, and he remembered the feel of her small, soft hand in his. *She speaks like a lady; her hands are soft and manicured. What is she doing here? Why is she a serving maid?* Questions reeled in his head.

"Excuse me, sir."

Dazed, David blinked up at the footman who served the fruit compote, then discreetly slipped a piece of paper into his hand and moved on.

David excused himself politely and left the table. Once in the hall, he read the note. *Meet me at the servant's entrance immediately.* No signature. He burned with curiosity as he hurried along the hallway. How very odd. Was it Rosella? No, she would never step foot near the servant's door. Lucinda, perhaps? David reached the back hallway. In the dim light he could see a figure in the shadows.

A frail little woman stepped forward to greet him.

"Thank you for coming. I apologize, but this is a desperate situation. I have no one else to turn to, and they say you are a just man." The woman bowed her head. "My name is Pearl. Lucinda told me that you brought her from town this afternoon. I am Rosella's sister."

"Rosella's sister? I can assure you, madam, all between us has been most proper in every respect."

"I am in no way suggesting otherwise, Mr. Morgan."

"Then may I inquire how it is that you know Lucinda?"

"All I can say at this moment is that I am Lucinda's friend. I apologize for taking you from dinner, but time is of the essence. You are a stranger to me and Lucinda, but I understand you are well thought of by the judge and my sister. Lucinda is in danger, and I am helpless to do anything."

David came to full attention. "Danger? How? She arrived not two hours ago."

"The story is long and tragic. I shall try to give you only the briefest details. Please understand, sir, that Lucinda knows nothing of what I am about to tell you. For years, I thought it best she never know. Now my deceit could cost Lucinda her life."

She took a breath and hurried on. "Rosella and Marshall had a daughter, a beautiful child named

Meghan that Marshall was so taken with he failed to give Rosella the attention she demanded."

The frail woman looked stricken. "Twenty years ago today, at Rosella's insistence, I secretly spirited that child away to New York to a wealthy family who was desperate for a child. The couple paid a huge sum of money for her. They made Rosella a rich woman, so rich she didn't mind not knowing any details of the transaction. I became nanny to that child, Meghan. The couple renamed her Lucinda. As she grew, she looked more and more like Rosella. Certainly you have noticed the strong resemblance. Twelve years ago, the family moved to Chicago, and for Lucinda's safety, I told them the truth. It frightened them so, they took Lucinda to England. She married the earl of Northland, and just over a year ago, he died. Lucinda and her parents returned to Chicago."

Pearl paused and wiped the tears streaming over her cheeks. She hastily summed up the story of the fire and Lucinda's financial situation. "Left with nothing, Lucinda chose to make a new beginning. Do you understand the danger of her being here? If my sister recognizes her. . ." She looked up, pure terror reflected in her eyes.

David stared. He most certainly understood the peril. If Rosella so willingly sold her child, then how far would she go to keep her secret? "What do you want from me?"

"I have no plan, sir. But Rosella is no fool. Even disguised in that horrid uniform, Lucinda's identity will be obvious. Rosella loves Marshall, but she is beauty to his beast. She will not allow anyone or anything to come before her. Lucinda inherited her mother's great beauty, and Rosella will make certain Marshall does not see his daughter. Ever."

Icy fingers of dread squeezed David's heart. The torment hiding in the judge's eyes finally made sense. So did the melodrama Rosella had staged on this date every year since he had known her. David's first inclination was to dash into the serving pantry, grab up Lucinda, and flee far and fast.

He spoke in an urgent whisper. "A new storm has begun. I can't take her away tonight without someplace to go. So how do we keep her hidden until morning?" David chastised himself. Ordinarily he could solve any predicament with a logical plan. But he had never faced a problem of this magnitude. His thoughts tumbled over each other and refused to be ordered.

Pearl's look told him she had no answers. "You must get back, now." She touched his arm before she scurried along the hall and disappeared through the fanning doors.

David started back to the dining room, his mind

churning. What if the judge wasn't as drunk as he pretended? David was a successful lawyer because he seemed to have a sixth sense. Maybe he felt the unrest in the house. He had been uneasy all evening but had chosen to ignore it. Now he had to get Lucinda hidden. But where? How?

Entering the dining room through the serving door, he returned to his seat. At the end of the table, the judge was deep in conversation; he didn't look up, but David had the distinct feeling he had been missed. His dinner partner immediately turned to him and launched into a new story as though he'd never left. David glanced toward the drawing room. *Please, Rosella, don't come through those doors.*

Lucinda spotted David halfway along the table, sitting with a coquettish older woman who never seemed to stop talking even while eating. The princeliest man at the table, David had on a beautifully tailored tuxedo that showed his broad shoulders to their best advantage. Though Lucinda tried subtly to attract his attention, he seemed unaware of her efforts. His faraway look told her that his thoughts were elsewhere. Reluctant to leave, she picked up a tureen and backed through the door to the hall, only to bump into Molly. "Lucy, you best get a run on. Cook's screaming for your scalp." She rolled her eyes.

Lucinda rushed toward the kitchen, the aromas of food filling the hall. Unexpectedly, hunger overwhelmed her. Her knees started to buckle; she caught her balance against the wall inside the fanning doors. In a light-headed moment, she saw herself seated as David's dinner partner. Felt his eyes warm and loving as he lifted a spoon of soup to her lips. Their gazes linked and the warm soup trickled onto her tongue. . .

"You, be quick with this platter of lamb!" Mrs. Kidd screeched, shattering Lucinda's dream. She deposited the tureen on the mountain of dirty dishes and, under Mrs. Kidd's eagle eye, raced to lift the enormous silver platter. Concentrating, Lucinda picked up the platter without sending the slightest shimmer through the delicate rope of mint jelly decorating its edges. She caught the cook's slight smile of approval.

"Now hurry along," Mrs. Kidd added in a much kinder voice, but Lucinda had already cleared the top of the stairs, rushing as fast as her burden allowed toward the dining room. There, David waited to be served. And after dinner they would meet. Quivers of anticipation lightened her spirits.

Chapter 6

Mr. Button took the tray from Lucinda. "That will be all in the dining room tonight, Lucy. Molly will show you the way to the card room. Polish the furniture one last time. Then see that the tables are prepared for playing whist." He looked hard at her. "You know about whist?"

Lucinda curtsied. "Yes, Mr. Button," she said and groaned silently. She hadn't eaten since this morning, but there was no mention of food. She remembered those who had served her so faithfully and lamented that she had been raised to think of servants as having few needs. When she was again in a position to be served, she vowed to be a different mistress.

While she polished the Chippendale tea table until it gleamed in the candlelight, she thought of David. How, when, where would they meet? She placed whist cards and score sheets on each of the five gaming tables and arranged the chairs into more suitable conversation groupings. She surveyed her handiwork and, satisfied that all was in readiness, pulled the bell cord that signaled Mrs. Kidd in the kitchen. Soon Molly arrived with a Sheffield tray of teacups and a heavy silver teapot. She dashed back to the kitchen, leaving Lucinda to set out the tea service. That done, she scanned the room once more. Numerous candelabra and wall sconces cast a warm glow over the brocades and velvets, all in shades of golden peach. The fire in the large marble fireplace burned in silent and smokeless perfection. The slight fragrance of oriental incense added a hint of mystery. Everything was as ready as she knew how to make it.

In the Florentine mirror, Lucinda reviewed her appearance and looked carefully at her apron to be sure it was still clean. At least she had been allowed to wear her blue wool dress instead of a gray, shapeless maid's frock. She tucked the stubborn lock of copper hair under the giant mushroom cap and made sure her hidden necklace didn't show. Satisfied she was presentable, she turned from the mirror. Were those lights in the lane? Mistress Tillotson's coach perhaps?

Hurrying to the window, she pulled aside heavy lace

curtains and stared into the dark. *Oh my, that coach is having a sorry time in this snow and wind.* The coach and four, battered by the storm, drew up before the house. Down from the driver's box vaulted a dark figure carrying a ship's lantern to light the way. He leaned into the wind and struggled to reach the broad front steps of the baronial house.

Disregarding the driving snow, a woman called from the coach window. "Button! Where are you? Is there no one to answer the door?" Her voice shrilled above the wind.

The staff was busy serving dessert, so Lucinda went to answer the summons. She had survived dinner without being thrown out with the chickens. Could she now please a mistress who came late and screamed for assistance? She set her face in a smile and, with quick, efficient steps, hurried down the stairway to the front door. All the while the mistress was caterwauling at the top of her lungs.

Lucinda held the oversized door open enough to see the footman leap from the box. He opened and steadied the coach door against the wind. A second footman lifted Rosella Tillotson from inside the coach. Carrying her, he staggered against the driving snow and deposited her at the top of the steps.

Judge Tillotson came hurrying down the hall and

pulled the door wide open. The wind swept inside, blowing out the lamps and casting everything in darkness. Stepping into the doorway, the man with the lantern held it high to furnish light. The judge braved the storm and stepped outside to meet his wife. The wind flapped the tails of his long black coat and rearranged his cravat and hair. Mistress Tillotson, standing erect and as tall as her husband, presented her cheek for his kiss. His lips brushed the general vicinity as he reached to take her arm. She pushed him away.

His expression remained pleasant, but Lucinda noticed a muscle working along his jaw. He ushered Rosella into the foyer, but it was so shadowed Lucinda could see little of the large woman except for a square chin under the bill of the bonnet.

David came striding along the dark hallway with Mr. Button and Molly at his heels. Immediately, the butler ordered the candles in the wall sconces relit. He looked straight at Lucinda.

David stepped beside her. "I'll show her where the safety matches are, Mr. Button." With the briefest of nods at David, Button turned his full attention to the Tillotsons.

Taking Lucinda's arm, David set a breathtaking pace down the hallway and into the dimly lit drawing room. He sat her in a large wing-backed chair facing the fireplace.

"Stay here while I take the matches to Button." And he was gone.

Lucinda stared in the fire. What in the world made David whisk her away like that? If he didn't have a good reason, they were going to have words. Just because she was a servant girl didn't mean she would allow such treatment. She had been assigned to the game room, and she was going to be on duty there whether David liked it or not. Dinner would soon be over, and the guests would be adjourning to the game room. What would Mistress Tillotson do when no one was there to serve? As Mr. Button threatened, Lucinda would be out with the chickens for sure. She was ready to leave when the door opened and closed.

"Lucinda?" David whispered.

She leaned around the chair so he could see her. "I'm here, but now that you're here, I must leave."

"I've brought Pearl to see you."

"Pearl?" Lucinda started to stand.

"Please, sit down." David's words were gentle as he pulled up a chair for Pearl and knelt beside Lucinda. "Pearl has something she needs to tell you. It will help you understand many things."

"What is going on? David, I won't be ordered around like this."

Pearl took Lucinda's hand and gave her a weak smile. "I'm so sorry. I should have told you years ago, but I never imagined anything like this would, could ever happen."

Chills ran up Lucinda's spine. "I don't think I want to hear this."

Pearl looked deep into Lucinda's eyes. "And I don't want to tell you, but you must know." When Pearl finished her story, Lucinda sat silent. "I hope you can forgive me." She hung her head and stepped back beside the fireplace.

Lucinda felt as if she had been pitched off a cliff and sent spinning toward huge rocks at the bottom. She gasped, but her lungs refused to fill. David rubbed her back. "Breathe in," he said softly. "That's right, another breath." She heard his voice as from a distance until her breathing stabilized and she could speak. "This is going to take time to sort out, Pearl. But I love you and hold nothing against you."

Pearl kissed Lucinda and held her for a moment. "I must get back to the laundry. David is a good lad. He'll see to your safety."

The door clicked shut, and David moved to the chair Pearl vacated. "The problem is keeping you safe through the night until we can put together a plan for getting you away from here."

"No matter if Rosella does recognize me, she'll be as shocked as I am. I'll be safe for a while yet." She slumped back in the chair. "Could I rest just a minute before I go upstairs?" Her eyes drooped from weariness.

He nodded, and her lids closed.

When voices filtered into the room from the hall, Lucinda woke. She felt brittle, as though if she were touched she would shatter into myriad slivers of glass. She felt the urge to scream and to go on screaming until she broke. Instead, she stood, her hands balled into fists at her side, and willed herself to complete the task at hand. "They are on the way to the game room. I must go."

"Come with me," David said. "I'll show you a way to the card room that will keep anyone from noticing your arrival."

Holding her hand, he led the way to a large mirror on the fireplace wall. He touched the heavy gold frame, and the mirror swung open. Lucinda gasped. "What, how. . . ?" she stammered.

"This house was used to hide runaway slaves during the War between the States. This is the hidden stairway they used." He helped her through the opening, closed the mirror, lit a small lamp, and led her up stairs that eventually came out at a panel in the library next to the card room.

"You go in. Busy yourself like you've been there all the time. I'll go back down and come up the main stairs."

When Lucinda arrived in the card room, Mistress Tillotson was waiting across the room at the top of the main stairway. She had changed clothes and wore a peignoir of white satin, flounced at the throat and covered with heavy lace at the waist. A double rope of pearls and diamonds lay across her ample bosom. Her amber hair was locked in a careless chignon held in place by a white net. *So, that is my mother.*

Thankfully, the mistress couldn't see her. Lucinda picked up a tray of champagne, and, staying as far from the woman as possible, began passing it to the guests. Mixing among them, she felt safe until she felt a tap on her shoulder. Keeping her head down, Lucinda turned. Rosella tipped her face up. The attempt to stifle her gasp failed. She continued to stare with a look of unclothed astonishment little different from those registered by David Morgan and Mr. Button. *She recognizes me!*

Lucinda kept her face frozen. "Champagne, mistress?" Her voice sounded normal, the English accent firmly in place.

Rosella, on the other hand, turned deathly pale, and her chest heaved for breath. "What is your name?" she gasped through trembling lips.

"Lucinda, ma'am." She carefully balanced the tray and curtsied. Over Rosella's shoulder, she saw David's eyes widen. He turned as pale as Lucinda felt.

Rosella's eyes narrowed. "Come," she said in a shrill voice and led the way to a card table. Her hand trembled as she picked up the deck of cards. "Now, my dears," she said to the three men present, "if you don't mind playing with my personal maid and secretary, we can begin."

Lucinda gasped. "Mistress, I–I. . . ," she stammered.

"You do play whist, do you not?" Her tone was sarcastic.

"I have played some," she said quietly.

"I do not wish to play this evening," Rosella announced. "You will be the fourth at my table."

The looks on the men's faces told what they thought of the idea. "Really, Rosella, this is too much," one of the men objected. "We came to play with you." The others at the table echoed his sentiments.

Mistress Tillotson ran an unsteady hand over her brow. "Very well, gentlemen, but don't expect much of me. It has been a long and most trying day." She looked squarely at Lucinda before she sat down and began shuffling the cards. "Lucinda, put that tray down."

"Yes, ma'am." Lucinda curtsied and handed off the tray.

"Make yourself useful in the library." Rosella began dealing the cards expertly, watching Lucinda all the while. "There are newspapers there. Find some bits of scandal to amuse me tonight when you prepare me for bed. See if you can find a novel, a love story, something set in India." She had regained her color and her voice, but her smile was brittle, her eyes hard. "And David, you are a poor player. Sit at my elbow and learn."

He sent Lucinda a look of resignation and seated himself beside Rosella.

Lucinda managed to stuff the feelings aroused by knowing that Rosella was her mother, but her movements were too sharp, too quick. She smiled at the right times and answered politely, but she was off-key, like an out-of-tune piano. She could tell David was worried. His eyes were overly bright and, to the detriment of his attention to the card game, he often gazed after her. That made her task more difficult because she wanted to look at him, but she forced herself to concentrate on the black print. In the *Peoria Review* and *Chicago Democrat* she found items she thought might interest Rosella. She finished her task, but the card party showed no sign of ending. After building up the fire in the card room's fireplace, Lucinda again moved to the library and examined the shelves for a novel to fit Rosella's description.

Attracted by the title *The Ganges by Moonlight,* she drew a volume from its place. As she did so, a leather pouch hidden behind the books slid out, scattering its contents.

Lucinda stood stock still, staring at the floor. "What is this?" Her heart leaped at the sight.

A handful of cut, unset jewels—emeralds, sapphires, two large rubies, and diamonds of various shapes and sizes—splattered over the Persian carpet. She stooped and was gathering them up when Rosella Tillotson came into the room with David at her heels, his face creased with concern. Rosella's eyes instantly focused on the sparkling stones in Lucinda's hand.

The briefest of smiles brushed Rosella's lips, then the expression vanished and her face became unreadable as she walked with firm steps across the room to where Lucinda stood, her trembling hands cupped around the jewels.

"How fortunate that you found my little gems. I had quite given them up for lost." Rosella's hands closed like icy claws over Lucinda's and grasped the stones. Her red mouth smiled, but her eyes were dark and hard.

Chapter 7

It was well past midnight before the guests were bedded and Lucinda was able to light her own candle to carry up to her attic room. The flame flickered in the sudden drafts and sent writhing shadows over the unfamiliar stair walls. She closed the door at the foot of the attic stairs and slid the little lock into place. Her room under the eaves was directly above Rosella's dressing room.

Though there was a bell to call for service, Rosella insisted on this arrangement because she preferred to rouse her maid during the small hours of the night by throwing a shoe at the ceiling, Lucinda had been told. She was ordered to listen for the thud beneath her bed and consider her position at the mansion to be dependent on her instant response to such a summons.

From kitchen maid to personal servant to the mistress—

her mother. So much had happened this day.

Lucinda stumbled with weariness on the last step and pitched the candle forward onto the splintered floor. It guttered out. The storm had passed for now. Through a single dormer window set in the slanted roof over her bed, moonlight flooded into the tiny cubicle and fanned across the tied patchwork quilt. Kneeling on the bed made from a knotty plank, she let the moon bathe her in white light. Warmth from an unseen source seemed to envelop her, bringing with it a longing for the way things were before catastrophe became an almost constant companion.

Thoughts of Rosella tried to rise, but Lucinda forced them away. She was far too weary to examine the latest blow to her life. *I never dreamed I would be grateful for such poor lodgings, but tonight I am. I am gifted with my own room.* The other maids slept in a long room under the eaves of another wing of the house. There were two rows of beds and no privacy.

Lucinda sat on the bed and caressed the platinum heirloom fastened around her neck. This was her only physical tie to her past. The memories it kindled would help her through the rough places. Surrendering to a consuming weariness, she scarcely managed to hang her apron and hat neatly on the peg beside her coat and cap. She brushed out her hair but chose to sleep in her dress in case she was summoned in the night.

Just when exhaustion should have sent her slipping under the quilt, she became caught up by a strange sensation she could neither capture nor dismiss. In that moonlit moment, Lucinda knew that she would not be a servant all her days. One day she would again have her own mansion filled with servants. And she would be waited on as she had served others tonight. *Is this the vision Yarrow Woman had of me?*

She eased her aching body under the quilt and onto a harsh covering over a thin horse blanket used for a mattress. The narrow bed might have been as soft as eiderdown for all she noticed. Staring up into the night through the window, her mind drifted away to mingle with the stars that shone like the jewels she had held in her hands. One day she would again have piles of beautiful gemstones. She thought about how Mistress Rosella, her mouth twisted, her eyes hard, had snatched the jewels and clutched them to her bosom. Lucinda would not clutch her jewels. She would have so many she could be, would be, generous.

Her thoughts turned to David Morgan sitting beside Rosella in the card room. *He was looking at me, only me.*

Lucinda's mind slipped further into the stars and saw that David stood alone on the veranda of a silver mansion glittering in the noon sun. She advanced toward him, bearing a heavy ornate tray. On it, instead of drinks, was a lumpy sack of silver and a neat stack of papers, stark white with black writing and large official seals. He helped himself to a stack and motioned to her to do the same. She set the tray down and took a few papers. He shook his head and handed her the whole stack. She fanned the sheets. They turned to silver coins falling like snow on the floor until she stood in a knee-deep drift. For no apparent reason, she woke up.

Her heart altered its pace and pounded a different rhythm in her ears. Her eyelids would not stay closed, fluttering instead like insistent moths. Nothing in the house below suggested an intruder, yet she believed someone to be about. She thought of the door at the bottom of her stairs. The simple lock would keep no determined soul out, but it would sound its own rattling alarm were someone to set hand to it.

Lucinda tensed and listened and knew with an unexplainable certainty that somewhere in the bowels of the sleeping house someone was awake and abroad. She slid from beneath the quilt and rose to her knees, searching for the latch on the slanted window over her head. Her fingers found and flipped open the latch. She broke the seal on the frame and tried to avoid the shower of dislodged grit and dead flies. Standing on her bed, she thrust back the window and straightened into the opening.

The air, tinged with the smell of evergreens, hung unmoving. Chimney pots belching occasional wisps of smoke stood over the house in rigid ranks like guards. Yes, she could climb out onto the roof and escape if it became necessary.

Relieved, she slid back through the window. Her feet, freezing now, found the bed below. She pulled the window closed and twisted the latch shut. Brushing off the debris and curling into the quilt, she shivered, not so much from cold as from the disturbing feeling that would not leave. At last, exhaustion overtook her and she slept.

For the second time that night, Lucinda sat bolt upright. A thud beneath her bed had wakened her. She struggled to remember where she was and finally realized Rosella had summoned her. Still caught in the web of a dream she could not remember, she moved as if in a trance across the cold, splintery floorboards toward the stairs. In the blackness of the stairway, her bare feet found their footing.

Loosed from its efficient knot, her curly hair tumbled over her shoulders and down her back. At the foot of the stairs, she twisted the lock, tripped the cold latch, and pushed open the door. Her bare feet sank into the oriental carpet runner along the hall leading to Mistress Tillotson's bedroom suite. Her hair blew across her face as air currents from the hallways below rose past her and into the attic.

A beam of moonlight struck the face of a floor clock. The time stood at three.

Lucinda turned the corner and entered an unlit hallway. She moved slowly along the corridor until she felt the doorframe and realized that she faced Mistress Tillotson's sitting room door. Her heart pounded in her throat, and her mouth dried with fear. She reached for the knob.

Someone came unheard from behind, and a hand gripped her shoulder. Lucinda's mouth opened to scream, but only a pitiful whimper escaped. *I shall be murdered,* she thought with terrifying clarity as the soft hand with fingers like steel bands tightened on her shoulder near her throat.

The black hallway seemed rent by screams, but when the man spun her around, she realized the sounds were all in her head. The dam in her throat prevented any communication. His hand easily held both of hers in a vise behind her back, and he pulled her to him, half-smothering her against his chest.

The sleeve against her throat was silky, and he smelled of sweet pipe tobacco. His cheek rested against her temple. "Oh, my beautiful one," he whispered. "Please don't fight me. I only want to hold you. I would never hurt you. Never. I will protect you. Care for you. Love you." A hand closed behind her neck, beneath her flowing hair. "Such magnificent hair, such perfect features." He caressed the flowing strands. "Do not be afraid. No one will hurt you. I promise."

Who was this man? Lucinda could not force her eyes open to look, shut tight in terror as they were. *None of this is happening.* Her exhausted mind and body refused to function further. She sank into a stupor, too stunned for thought or prayer, too frightened to call for help.

Then, as suddenly as he came, he vanished without a sound.

Tears flooded her cheeks. Lucinda's shaking hand gripped the chair molding along the hallway, and soundlessly she started back along the corridor. Before she turned the corner, she looked back. In the deep shadows, she watched a short man open the door to Rosella's bedroom. He stood for several seconds silhouetted in the glow cast by fire from the hearth of the bedroom fireplace. Then, as though having been invited, he stepped across the threshold into Rosella Tillotson's bedroom and carefully shut the door.

Lucinda fled up the narrow stairs to her attic and

curled into her bed. With cold, trembling fingers she sought the comfort of her necklace.

It was gone.

A sob escaped, and a stupefying emptiness swept over her. Yarrow Woman's words drummed in her head, *"Never take it off or let anyone else take it from you."* Yet Lucinda could not bring herself to go back down those stairs. Even though her mistress summoned her, she could not go. A deep moaning sob escaped, shook her body. She knotted her fist at her throat and cried over her loss until she fell into a deep sleep.

Chapter 8

Lucinda woke with a startled cry, roused violently from more violent dreams. Strong hands muffled her mouth as someone ripped the quilt from her trembling body. She struggled against her assailant and fought for breath.

"Hush, Lucinda!" a strong, deep voice pleaded urgently. "It's David Morgan come to save you. Stay still!" The hovering form removed his hand from her mouth.

Shouts and the clatter of the bolted door at the foot of the stairs rent the night.

"What are you doing here?" she gasped. "What do I need to be saved from?" It was then that the scene in the hallway spun up through her exhaustion-fogged brain. Was that awful person trying to get at her again? How would David know?

The sound of wood splintering meant the door was giving way under the assault. He shoved her feet into the brogans. "Hurry! Up through the window. Those shoes are bound to be slick. Watch your footing on the roof."

His voice was rough as he helped her into her coat and hat and hoisted her through the opening. Far below, the yard was still darkly quiet, but footfalls pounded on the stairs behind them. David crept out onto the roof and stood beside her. Lucinda burrowed into his sheltering arms and pressed her face hard into his chest as though he could make the terror go away.

"Stay low," he said softly. Hugging the shadows, he steered her along the roof. Her shoes slipped on the cold tiles, but David held her tight and kept her moving.

"Watch your step on the ladder," he whispered. "I'll go first and guide your feet onto the rungs." He pried her hand from his, and the parting wrenched her heart. With the greatest care, he placed each foot on the rung, but still she never felt more gratitude than when she stepped onto the ground. He pulled her into the deep shadows of shrubs next to the house. "Wait here."

Taking down the ladder, he laid it against the foundation and came back to her.

Lucinda fought tears. "David, can't you tell me what's going on? Who are those men? Why are they chasing us?"

He motioned her to silence and rushed them through the shadows along the side of the house.

A horse whinnied.

He pulled her to her knees and knelt before her, shielding her body from any eyes. "Catch your breath. I know you didn't do anything, but we have to keep you from that pack of ruffians the judge has set on you. Do you understand that?"

"No, I don't understand any of this, but I trust you." She set her lips in a line and swiped two large tears tracking down her cheeks. David stood, wrapped her in his great arms, and pulled her to her feet. "The entrance to the secret stairs is inside the yew hedge." He glanced right, left, and behind like a cornered fox. "All right, run!"

They fled across the lane and inside the thick hedge. He took a branch and swept away their footprints, then lifted the trap door. Once inside the tunnel, he struck a safety match and lit the small oil lamp. "This is used often by servants returning late." He grinned. Making sure the trapdoor was secured, he led the way through the tunnel and up the hidden stairway inside the house.

It seemed an eternity before she was once again sitting in the drawing room, now dark except for what was left of the fire's faint embers casting a glow on the area directly before the hearth. David spread a lap rug over her. "I'm hoping this is the last place anyone would think to look for you. I need to get my letter and money."

"Please, David, I don't understand any of this."

"I'll be right back and will tell you everything."

Lucinda heard the door latch click shut, and her heart sank. Too tired and frightened to think, she stared into the embers of the hearth for what seemed hours until once more the door opened and someone—no, more than one—came into the room. She held her breath. Footsteps came toward the fireplace. *Dear Father in heaven, help me, help me,* she prayed over and over.

"It's David," he whispered. "And Pearl." He set his leather case beside the fireplace.

"Did you say 'Pearl'?"

Pearl came into view and set two small bags beside David's. She bustled over to Lucinda. "You need looking after, and I don't want to spend the rest of my days in the laundry press. I'm coming with you." She stood bundled inside her coat.

Lucinda looked at the bags. "Where are we going? Please tell me what's happening. I can't imagine why I'm being pursued."

David knelt beside her. "Earlier this evening Mistress Tillotson was found assaulted in her dressing room. The gemstones she took from you are missing. The judge said she was clutching a shoe in one hand and your antique necklace in the other. Thus, my dear Lucinda, it is you they are seeking."

Lucinda's hand flew to her throat. Panic rushed over her. "I had it on," she cried. Her heart raced and she felt sick. "How did the judge get it?" Then, she remembered the man who accosted her in the hallway. She told David the story.

"Your account of the man who waylaid you describes the judge. He must have taken the necklace from you and later placed it in Rosella's hand. I wondered how he even knew about it." David reached in his pocket and laid her necklace, the emeralds gleaming, on her lap.

Lucinda caressed the jewels. "David, how did you get this?"

"It was on my bed wrapped in a silk handkerchief like the ones the judge carries."

"I don't understand."

"I think he figured out that Rosella arranged for you to be kidnapped twenty years ago. He confronted her with his suspicions. Whatever she said or did made him so angry that he grabbed the poker and hit her, though he didn't kill her. Afraid for you, he planted the necklace he took, knowing that would force you to flee. She is still unconscious, but Pearl overheard Rosella tell the judge she'd take care of you herself this time and know the job was done right. Since he saw us talking together earlier in the salon, I suspect he counted on Pearl and me helping you to get away. It's snowing hard and our tracks will soon be covered." He checked his watch. "Things are finally getting quiet, but dawn will soon be here. We don't have much time."

Lucinda's thoughts were spiraling. "Where are we going?"

"To Yarrow Woman."

"Why to her?"

"Her name is Mary Margaret Mason," David explained. "She was captured by the Indians when she was fifteen. The Masons moved heaven and earth and spent a fortune to get her back. She fought returning to her old world, having become more Indian than white. Now she lives on the edge of the Mason property. She dresses as an Indian, talks their language, and has little to do with anyone but the prairie settlers. Hers is the perfect place to hide until we can figure out what to do." David looked outside. "I'll get the sleigh and Kambur. You and Pearl wait at the tunnel exit. I'll come back for you shortly."

And he was gone.

Chapter 9

From Illinois to Kansas the prairie stretched miles without number, a gray wasteland filled with empty silence and boundless cold. A hard wind from the northwest pushed across the flatland, but in this deep fold of earth, it was calm. David pulled the sleigh to a halt in front of Yarrow Woman's cabin. He had heard many stories of this strange woman, but he tried not to believe them.

The slab door creaked open, and David hoped they weren't going to be looking down the barrel of a shotgun. Showing no signs of surprise, Yarrow Woman motioned them in. "Hurry, all of you."

David didn't need a second invitation. He helped the two women out of the sleigh, and they entered the dusky interior, a small room that served as Yarrow Woman's kitchen, parlor, and dispensary. Shelves lining the walls were filled with bottles and vials. A blend of aromas wafted from bunches of dried herbs hung from the rafters. In the kitchen area a small cooking stove occupied the corner next to the copper sink, which had an indoor water pump. Kerosene lamps on the windowsills and the round oak table gave off a yellow glow. Yarrow Woman sat Pearl and David at the table and Lucinda in a willow rocker near the fireplace. Two gray cats on the hearthstones stirred and coolly examined Lucinda with their green eyes.

Yarrow Woman also studied Lucinda. "You arrived at the Tillotsons' in time."

Lucinda managed a wan smile. "I did, and as you predicted, I served a very short time."

David wondered how much Yarrow Woman had already guessed but told her the whole story, anyway.

"I've been waiting for you." She smiled. "The hens are laying well. I will whip us up an omelet." Without waiting for a response, she busied herself at the kitchen counter.

"We apologize for placing you in such danger, but we had nowhere else to turn," David explained.

She brought them steaming mugs of coffee. "I have been thinking of what we can do. I have spent far too many years baking scones and listening to the troubles of settlers. My bones tell me it is time to go home." The room grew silent. "Come, Lucinda, you must eat. I doubt they fed you at the Tillotsons'."

David bounded to his feet and helped her to the table. His heart ached when he looked at her. She was pale, and dark circles ringed her eyes.

Yarrow Woman came carrying a silver serving tray. After the blessing, they feasted on the omelet and generous slices of bread.

"Lucinda, you are almost asleep," Yarrow Woman said when they finished the meal. "Let me tuck you into bed while we pack the sleigh." She guided the exhausted girl to the bed in the adjoining bedroom.

While Yarrow Woman filled boxes with food and bottles with water, she directed Pearl in filling several gunny sacks with herbs. David laid fresh straw over the bed of the sleigh and stacked up bales of hay for the horses. The food and water he padded with quilts and pillows. Finished, they sat down for a last cup of coffee and some elk jerky.

A mighty crash thundered against the door.

They leaped out of their chairs.

The door exploded open.

David stared into cruelty: a middle-aged man with a red beard on a skeletal face glared at them from behind a

Remington shotgun. A white scar zigzagged down his cheek, pulling his mouth into a perpetual sneer. Nothing in his expression suggested goodness or mercy. Cold, black eyes raked the room.

David, his insides knotted, forced himself to stay calm. "Who?"

"Don't try to stall me. I ain't stupid. Where is the new maid what tried to kill the judge's wife? The judge wants her real bad."

"I don't know about a new maid trying to kill anyone."

"Word's spread over the county. New maid hired yesterday disappeared from the Tillotson place sometime after midnight. Old judge is paying a thousand dollars silver for her return alive, no questions asked."

David couldn't believe the judge would post a reward. He knew Lucinda was his daughter and would want her safe. Tillotson servants must have seen easy money in the return of Lucinda, David guessed, and exploited the situation. "Do you have a wanted poster or anything to prove your story?" David stepped toward the antsy gunman.

He shifted the weathered shotgun and pointed it directly at David's midsection. "Word I got is straight from someone at the mansion. Countryside's crawlin' with bounty hunters. Nobody's thought to look here yet."

This fellow probably wasn't a bounty hunter. Under

the brim of his greasy hat, sweat beaded on his forehead, and his hand holding the gun twitched nervously. His desperation and lack of experience, however, made him more dangerous.

His ugly bearded face took on a sly look. "I says to myself, I says, I'll just have a look around the squaw's place." He brandished the gun at Yarrow Woman, but she didn't move a muscle. "And look what I find. A sleigh at the front door and three innocent-looking people with nothin' in common, getting' ready to leave." He pointed his gun at the boxes and sacks stacked in the corner. His laugh was low and coarse. "Wonder where the fourth one is?" Keeping the gun trained on them, he began a thorough search of the room, including looking through all the drawers and cupboards and tapping the walls and floors for signs of hidden closets or trapdoors.

David spoke up. "As you can see, there are no hiding places here."

The ruffian looked toward the bedroom. "That must mean you got her stowed away in the other room." His heavy boots thumped on the floor as he walked to the door.

David's heart turned over. There was no place in that room to hide. *Think, David, think. You have to do something.* He turned toward the fireplace and the poker resting there. The man whirled and leveled the gun. "See the notches on the butt?" David could. "You wanna be another one?"

He would be no good to anyone if he were dead. David froze, but his heart raced.

The old hunter unlatched the door and eased it open with the toe of his boot. Silently the door swung open to reveal a single bed spread with a tan Indian blanket in the corner of the small room. On the opposite wall stood an ornate mahogany armoire with a large mirror beside it. A small table next to the bed and a single willow chair completed the furnishings. The floor was bare pine slabs; a large rag rug lay rolled up in front of the armoire. The thug pulled open the muslin curtains covering the single window and looked out over the snowy yard.

Oh, dear God in heaven, don't let him look down, David prayed. A small scrap of blue fabric hung from a nail on the side of the window. *Lucinda! She has more courage than anyone I know. But where is she hiding out there in the wind? She'll freeze.*

Apparently convinced Lucinda was still in the house, the ugly man looked under the bed and poked the mattress with the gun barrel. Nothing. He turned his attention to the armoire. After checking every drawer, he then gave the rug a solid kick with the side of his boot, thumped it with the butt of his gun, shrugged, and went about tapping walls and floor for hollow sounds. He found nothing. He rested his foot on the rug and snarled, "I know ya got her stashed somewheres." He bent down and started to unroll the rug.

David clenched his fists and wished he hadn't packed his pistol away in the wagon. Pearl turned her back and clamped her hand over her mouth. Yarrow Woman's face remained stoic, but her black eyes sparked rage.

The rug flopped open. Nothing. He swore his disappointment. "Well, folks, she cain't stay hidden ferever. I'll just wait it out."

David stormed through the doorway, his hands working, his breath coming hard and fast. "Your search is over. Get out!"

The man thrust the gun in David's face. "Lucky fer you I'm feelin' generous, or you'd be dead. But shoot you I will. It'll give me pleasure to let you stew not knowin' when." His look included them all. "I'll be watchin'."

He tromped outside, waved his fist in the air, and yelled obscenities at David, who stood in the doorway with Yarrow Woman's gun trained on the man. The old scoundrel mounted his horse and rode out of range. He stopped and hung his leg around the saddle horn, making it plain he was prepared to wait out their departure.

They rushed to the window and threw open the sash. "Lucinda," David called softly. Her face appeared around the corner of the house. "Come, we'll help you in." She grasped the rope David lowered and hung on tight while he hoisted her up and into the room. "Lucinda, oh, Lucinda, are you all right?"

She looked up into his eyes, and he caressed her face and hair. "How brave you are. That's a long drop to the ground. Are you hurt?"

"I don't think so. Just terribly cold."

Yarrow Woman pushed David out of the way. "I'll tend to Lucinda. You finish with the sleigh."

David tied Kambur to the rear of the buckboard sleigh and checked the traces of Yarrow Woman's gray Percheron. Satisfied that all was well, he took off his oilskin and climbed into the sleigh. Yarrow Woman appeared, and they quickly stretched a canvas top over a frame to keep out the worst of the storm and block the view of the front door.

"Pearl, you get in. We'll get Lucinda."

They wrapped her in the rug. David picked up one end and Yarrow Woman the other. Gently they carried her to the wagon. Pearl guided the burden inside until it rested on the straw.

"Can you breathe all right?" David asked. He was thankful to hear a muffled yes. He leaned the front door in place and climbed up on the seat beside Yarrow Woman. A mewing caught his attention. Beside her on the floorboard was a basket containing her two cats. *She's such a softy under that rough exterior.*

"I'm glad you know the way," he said to Yarrow Woman.

She nodded and slapped the reins, and they were off. When they reached the prairie, David looked back. A solitary horseman followed close enough to be seen.

Minutes later, David looked back again. *He's still there and drawing closer. He's going to do exactly as he said. We're all going to be dead before nightfall except Lucinda.* He couldn't even think about what would happen to her.

By mid-afternoon, David realized the man was not going away. Up the road, another snow squall stalled and waited for them to drive into a whiteout.

They were almost out of time, but David still had no idea what to do. After they drove into the whiteout, he had Yarrow Woman stop. He crawled into the back and got his gun. He untied Kambur and mounted up. "Go on. I'll catch up," he shouted over the wind.

He rode to the edge of the whiteout and waited. It wasn't long until the hunter rode by, his head bent against the blizzard. He had let down his guard. David waited until he passed, then followed him. The wind carried away all sound. David rode up beside him. He cocked his pistol and pointed it at the man's head.

"Hands in the air!" he shouted. David reached over and lifted the shotgun out of the old man's raised hands. He pitched it far out into the whiteness. Searching through the man's pockets, he found a pair of handcuffs. David cuffed his hands, turned the horse around, and with a solid boot to the rump, sent the horse galloping back the way it had come.

David felt no remorse as he turned around and again faced the wall of white. The bounty hunter wouldn't die, and he couldn't hurt Lucinda anymore. David sat very still, with no idea of which way to go. Letting the reins go slack and with a prayer on his lips, he allowed Kambur to move forward on his own.

The storm had stopped by the time David spotted Yarrow Woman's sleigh before a sod house with an attached stable. Another sleigh stood in the yard. David leaped down from Kambur and made his way to the door, realizing that this must be the "inn" Yarrow Woman had referred to earlier. Tacked there was a sign: DIPHTHERIA. His heart sank.

"Hey, there," a voice called from near the stable. "Praise be to God! We're having a baby. Your friends are inside the stable helping my wife."

David turned and recognized Andy Henderson, the Tillotsons' former head groomsman.

Chapter 10

The stable was quiet. Lying on beds of fresh straw and wrapped in buffalo robes, the weary travelers encircled the makeshift fire pit. Andy kept watch over Gigi and baby Gabriel asleep in her arms. The animals rested in stalls beyond the flickering firelight.

Unable to sleep, Lucinda sat up and stared into the fire. "This is the most amazing Christmas I've ever had, but I feel as though something more will happen," she said to no one in particular.

"It has been a sacred experience," Pearl agreed and rolled to a sitting position.

David roused up and looked puzzled. "It does seem incomplete, somehow. I, too, feel like I'm waiting for something more."

"Maybe that's why I don't want the night to end."

Lucinda felt David's loving eyes on her, and they smiled across the fire.

Soft drumbeats sounded from a dark stall at the back of the room. With great dignity, Yarrow Woman in her white buckskin dress with its heavy beaded designs, her dark hair in two thick braids down her back, came to the fire. She pulled up a log stump and sat. "Before we sleep this night, we must give thanks for this lowly stable as refuge from the storm and protection from the disease in the cabin beyond. Please bow your heads."

Lucinda closed her eyes and listened intently to the prayer. Yarrow Woman expressed all that was in Lucinda's heart and warmed her with peace and gratitude. When Yarrow Woman pronounced the amen, Lucinda and the others echoed it.

Again Yarrow Woman softly beat the little drum. "It is now Christmas Day. Would you like to hear the legend based on the birth of our Savior as told by my people?"

Lucinda's breath caught. Was this what they had been waiting for? "Yes. Oh yes." Her voice chimed in unison with the others.

"In the country north of us," Yarrow Woman began in her firm but soft voice, "there is the *he sapa,* a range of pine-covered mountains so green that from a distance they look black. At the foot of the *he sapa* are the mysterious *mako sica,* or Badlands, a mass of buttes and spires that stretch as far as the eye can see. The Badlands end at the sweeping prairie, long and wide and rolling. To the Northern Plains tribes who live there, all of creation—animals, birds, insects, plants, and humanity—are part of the sacred hoop. The Lakota express this as *mitakuye oyasin.*

"A very long time ago, the people who had been full of goodwill and generosity of spirit began to lose those virtues. The wise men were much concerned and fasted and prayed diligently to the Great Spirit for help. He heard their prayers and told the grandfathers to bring the people together on the longest night in the month of the moon.

"Out of curiosity, they came, hard of heart, selfish and arrogant, to wait and watch. They were not disappointed, for as the light darkened, they saw an eagle. It soared in high, wide circles above the Black Hills and out over the mysterious Badlands until the setting sun struck fire upon its wings. This was the signal, the grandfathers said. For what, they refused to say.

"The night settled like black velvet, and the people lit a huge bonfire. They encircled the fire and sat, watching the sparks rise among the stars. The air, cold and crisp, was scented with the sweet smoke. The night sky was radiant, the silence vast, peaceful, expectant.

"When the hush became so deep the titmouse could be heard, the representatives for *mitakuye oyasin* began to arrive—Those Who Fly and the Four-Leggeds—and take their place in the circle. They sat together around the glowing coals until all their heartbeats were as one.

"Then the snow goose stepped forward. 'The people have gone astray from the cycles of their journey and are lost. I will teach them the patterns of the seasons.'

"The chipmunk came to the fire. 'The Two-Leggeds wander, hungry and without purpose. I will teach them to gather and store the harvest. I will share my store of nuts.'

"The great buffalo lumbered up and stood with lowered head. 'The people waste what they take and share nothing. I will give my flesh to feed them and, to warm them, my coat. I will give myself away.'

"The eagle flew up and landed in the forming circle. 'The Two-Leggeds are blind. They do not see the aftermath of their actions. Perhaps if I give them my eyes, they will see beyond the present.'

"Each representative moved to the circle to tell of a gift, the most precious portion of themselves, that they wished to share until all had spoken and the night was silent again.

"When the very air quivered with anticipation, from inside the night came the deep, sad voice of the Creator.

'Those Who Fly and Four-Leggeds, you waste your-selves. They will accept your gifts and take the credit unto themselves.' There was heavy silence. 'It is I who must give myself. I will come, innocent and small.'

" 'How is that possible?' asked the relations." 'A Babe will be born, the Son of the Great Spirit. He will be born among the Four-Leggeds and Those Who Fly. He will give hope where there is hopelessness. He will bring love where there is hate. His name will be great among the people of the world.'

"And the people's hearts grew soft and loving. They looked at themselves and asked what they could give to the Small One. They were told they were free to give anything, anything at all, as long as the gift required the giver to make a great sacrifice.

"So the people went in search of perfect gifts to lay at the feet of the Small One. Some found their gifts at once; others searched longer; but many searched most of their lives before they found gifts perfect enough. Some never found a gift, because once more they strayed far from the virtuous life, the Red Road. The Small One was sad about that.

"On the longest night in the month of the moon, each gift was honored and the giver given a blessing and a promise. And for a little while, the people were once again full of goodwill and generosity of spirit.

"And so it is in our time, on the longest night in the month of the moon, we bring a perfect gift to somebody and give it in the name of the Small One. Tonight I give my gift—this drum given to me by the grandfathers, that I have cherished for many years—to Baby Henderson, in the name of the Small One, our Savior and Lord, Jesus Christ."

A holy silence filled the stable and was disturbed only by an occasional snap of an ember.

Lucinda remembered all the lavish Christmas celebrations and presents of her past. Nothing had stirred her heart like the message of this simple story. She fingered her necklace and thought how she had counted on it for her strength. It had become an idol to her! This knowledge came with a shock. *Do I have the faith to give it away?* It was a perfect gift and would help the young couple. She herself could never sell it for money. Giving it was truly a sacrifice.

She looked at David and found him studying her, his eyes filled with a love she had never known. As though he read her mind, he smiled and nodded.

Slowly, Lucinda returned the nod and sent her love to him. She understood. *I must trust God to take care of me and not depend on things.* With a prayer for strength to release the necklace and the past it represented, she slid from beneath the robe and knelt before Gigi. "In the name of the Small One, I give this necklace, cherished by generations of the House of North. It is the last tangible object from my past. It will become the foundation of the future for the House of Henderson." And she fastened the necklace around Gigi's neck.

Lucinda entered into the silence that once again settled over the stable as the gift was honored and the spirit of the season entered each heart.

Then David rose from his bed and walked to Kambur's stall. He returned with the bridle and saddle blanket, knelt, and laid them at Andy's feet. "Lucinda and I will be traveling west by train. We'll go as far as Nebraska, where I have something I must settle with my brother. After witnessing all that Lucinda has been through, all that she has suffered, I realize I have some fences I must mend. I need to find work and let Lucinda get to know me and my family."

"I would like that," she said quietly.

A broad smile lit his face, and he turned back to Andy. "You have a gift with horses, so I know you will treasure Kambur and take good care of him. If you choose to breed him, the charge for his services will support your family well. Kambur is a choice animal, and

I give him to you in the name of the Innocent One who left His heavenly home to come to earth and sacrifice Himself for us." He moved to sit beside Lucinda, cradling her in his arms.

Again the silence descended and deepened. Lucinda, safe now, felt the very air change. God's presence seemed to come into the stable to watch with approval. Soft tears streamed down her face, and her heart burned with joy.

The fire burned low. David stirred the coals and added a log. The smoke carried sparks up through the smoke hole in the roof and left the scent of apple wood inside the stable. He returned to his place beside Lucinda, and she leaned her head on his shoulder. He again put his arms around her and held her close. "You realize that all we have in this world is eighty dollars."

She smiled and dug into her coat pocket. "I have twenty-five cents. We are rich. Very rich."

They both looked over at Yarrow Woman. David then looked back at Lucinda and framed her face with his hands, kissing her gently, tenderly. "We are indeed rich beyond our grandest fantasies."

The straw rustled as Pearl pushed back her robe and stood. All eyes focused on her. "I have been praying to know what I should do. I have raised Lucinda from baby-hood, and she is like my own. But she is grown now and has found a wonderful man to love and who loves her. I need to let you go and make your own way."

Lucinda felt stricken. It had never occurred to her that Pearl would not want to be with her and David. "You're not leaving us for good, are you?"

"Never that." She smiled, kissed Lucinda, and crossed to where Gabriel lay. Dropping to her knees in front of the baby, she said, "I have no worldly possessions to bring, but I can give myself in service to the Lord by serving Gabriel and his family. Will you accept my gift?"

Andy and Gigi gaped at Pearl, and disbelief filled their eyes. Gigi finally found her voice. *"Oui, oui."*

"Then I shall see David and Lucinda safely to their destination in Nebraska and return to you by the time you are ready to travel."

Andy wiped away a tear and nodded. "We will love you, and you will have a home with us all the days of your life." He turned to David and Lucinda. "Earlier we discussed this. Gigi and I would like you to be godparents to our firstborn."

David and Lucinda nodded, unable to speak. Pearl hugged them both and then moved her bed next to the baby.

Yarrow Woman stood and raised her arms. "The circle is complete. We recognize that the true meaning of

Christmas is Christ's sacrificial birth, life, death, and resurrection for us. These gifts are our poor attempts to remind us of His great sacrifice and to show our gratitude for it. May the Spirit of the Lord abide with us this day and every day during the coming year. Amen."

EASY FRUIT COBBLER

$\frac{1}{2}$ cup butter

1 cup flour

1 cup sugar

$1\frac{1}{2}$ teaspoons baking powder

$\frac{3}{4}$ cup milk

2 cups fruit

1 cup sugar

Preheat oven to 350 degrees. Melt butter in oven in 9 x 9-inch pan. In bowl, mix flour, 1 cup sugar, baking powder, and milk. Blend well. Pour batter into pan with melted butter; don't stir. Pour fruit over the top and sprinkle with remaining 1 cup sugar. Bake 25 minutes. Serve hot with vanilla ice cream.

Maryn Langer descends from a long line of storytellers. She combines the history of the West with the romance of the heart. She gave her life to the Lord at an early age. He has shepherded her beside still waters and green pastures and through the valleys of temptation. Her prayer is that those who read her books will be entertained and reassured that there is a loving God who loves us and answers our prayers.

Epilogue

by Pamela Griffin and Maryn Langer

D avid helped Lucinda off the wagon and nodded to the driver. "I can't thank you enough."

A gap-toothed smile split the face of the elderly man, who'd introduced himself as Jebediah Meyers. "Well, now, I sure couldn't let you and your purty little bride sit at the train station when your chaperone left on the return train. Since I wuz headin' home anyway, it wasn't a problem."

David didn't bother to correct the man on his assumption that he and Lucinda were married. He hoped by spring they would be, and David greatly looked forward to that day. However, at this moment his stomach twisted in knots as if he'd overindulged in a six-course dinner. His brother was a stubborn man, not known for granting forgiveness once a wall had been built, and David had certainly built a thick one. Could he climb over it? Had he made a mistake in coming to this place?

Any courage he'd shown during their escape days ago felt just out of reach now.

Lucinda slipped her hand into his. "It will be all right. Yarrow Woman told us that God directs His people on which paths to take. I believe we have chosen the right course."

David nodded, though he heard the underlying tightness in her voice. Her palm felt moist, and he gently squeezed her hand.

"The people you're lookin' for live in that purty white timbered house over yonder," Jebediah said. "Cain't miss it." He laughed at his own joke, then flicked the reins on the mules' backs while making a clicking sound with his tongue for them to proceed. "Have yourselves a prosperous New Year, folks."

Once the wagon rattled away, David eyed the scarce town of Leaning Tree with its total of seven modest buildings, most of them sod. Jebediah was correct. Finding the right house wouldn't be difficult. He guided Lucinda over the snowy ground and up the few steps to the porch. Before he lost his nerve, he knocked loudly on the front door.

Seconds later, an exotic-looking woman with flowing black hair and gold hoops in her ears answered. She held a baby against her colorful dress.

David's greeting froze on his lips. Had he misunderstood Jebediah and approached the wrong house? He glanced at the few buildings to his right but saw nothing that resembled "white" or "timbered" or even "purty."

"I'm looking for Winifred Morgan—er, Pettigrass," he said. The driver had told him Winnie was married.

The woman only stared, a slight smile on her lips. She shook her head, as if to show she did not understand.

"Juanita, who is it?"

The familiar voice met David's ears. His breathing instantly felt constrained, and he struggled to retain his composure.

Winifred came into view, plumper and prettier than he remembered. Her blue eyes widened when she saw him, and she lifted her palms to her rosy cheeks. "Dai? Is that you?"

David hadn't heard his Welsh name in so long, he wasn't prepared for the emotion it evoked. He'd adopted the English version of the name Dai seven years ago when he turned his back on his older brother and went to Illinois intent on building his own life. Until this moment, he had not realized how horribly he missed his family. He felt Winifred's arms encircle him but seemed powerless to lift his.

"Come you inside. It is freezing." Quickly Winifred

215

ushered them into the house in time to hear what sounded like a plate crash to the floor. Running footsteps thudded against the wooden planks.

"Dai? My Dai's come back to me?" His mother rushed from the rear of the house.

Emotion cut off any possible words at the sight of her beloved wrinkled face. Sobbing, she approached and embraced him, and David was finally able to lift his arms. He held her and Winnie a long time. The women's tears soon mixed with gentle laughs and choppy phrases.

Suddenly David was aware of a stylishly dressed woman and a tall man walking down the corridor toward them. So engrossed were they in conversation that they didn't notice the reunion taking place in the entryway.

"Boston, I don't mind you buying things for our house, not one bit," the man said in amusement. "But don't you think you should wait 'til I build it first?"

The lovely woman's face flushed pink. "I can't help myself, Craig. The prospect of having our own home is so exciting. I had no idea that fifty dollars could go so far—beyond even what I bought for my family." She stopped suddenly, catching sight of David. "Oh, hello," she said curiously.

Winnie and his mother pulled back, blotting their faces with their fingers and laughing self-consciously.

Their gazes went beyond David and remained fixed. Suddenly, he realized why. With what he hoped was a look of contrition for forgetting her even for a moment, he held out a hand to his love. Lucinda moved forward, looking at David with understanding in her eyes before she turned them toward his family.

"Mother, Winnie, this is Lucinda. My fiancée."

His mother's eyes widened, and Winnie gulped in a nervous laugh. David tensed as his mother eyed Lucinda a long moment, paying particular attention to her ill-fitting coat and yellow-and-blue-striped cap. Then she smiled and moved forward to embrace her. "Welcome. Come, sit. I will fix us something hot to drink to warm you both up."

They made their way into the living room. The man stepped forward and held out his hand. "I'm Craig Watson, and this is my fiancée, Ivy. Welcome to Leaning Tree."

David shook his hand, but before he could introduce himself, Winifred blurted out, "This is Dai!"

"So, you're my stepfather's brother," Ivy murmured as she stood beside Craig and smiled. "It's a pleasure to meet you both," she said.

"Stepfather?" David asked.

"Mairwen passed on to glory three years ago,"

Winifred explained. "Our brother has remarried."

The brisk cold touched the back of David's neck as the door opened again. He turned. A fair-haired older child stood on the threshold next to a smaller girl with the same features.

"Ah, here are Gwen and Crystin," Winifred said. "Come then, girls. This is your uncle Dai."

Gwen's face immediately brightened. "Uncle Dai?" She rushed forward and hugged him hard around his middle, surprising David.

Crystin was less demonstrative, though she did smile. "Hello."

David swallowed over the lump in his throat. "Hello. You were only a baby when I last saw you. And your sister, here, had just turned six."

Suddenly a shadow from the doorway blocked the outside light. David looked up and tensed when he saw Gavin.

Gavin stood motionless. A woman came up beside him, looking like an older version of Ivy. Her dark brows drawn in apparent confusion, she looked at Gavin, then at the gathering.

"Gavin," Winifred finally said, nervousness evident in her tone. "Look who's come back to us. Our Dai has come home."

"Is this true now?" Gavin asked, his voice gravelly and deep. "Have you come home?"

David shared a look with Lucinda. Her green eyes encouraged him.

"For a short time, yes. I have the prospects of work in San Francisco. Lucinda and I plan to build our life there. I wanted to see everyone again. So we took the train. We found it imperative to leave Illinois." His lawyer's brain calculated recent facts, but the information seemed slow in reaching his mouth, and his words came out choppy.

Gavin nodded once. David tensed as his brother approached, then held out his work-worn hand. "You are welcome," Gavin said. "It is good to see you."

David felt rooted in shock, unable to shake his brother's hand. "It is?"

"Yes. I had much time to think, and perhaps I was wrong to expect you to follow my dream." Gavin looked toward their mother, then again at David. "You must follow your own dream."

David rapidly blinked back tears and tried to maintain control. When he was younger, he'd looked up to his older brother. He may not always have understood him, but he always loved him. And then that day on the dock. . .

"I said some horrible things," David croaked, feeling nineteen again. "I never should have struck you."

For the first time, Gavin smiled, and David saw the old familiar light of teasing in his eyes. "And perhaps I should not have struck back. Yes? Though your fresh mouth did deserve it."

Knowing that this was his brother's way of saying all was forgiven, David grinned and took Gavin's hand. They shook hands until Gavin pulled David into a fierce hug. Tears rolled down the faces of both men.

"Praise be to God!" David heard his mother exclaim. "At last, my prayers have been answered."

A Letter to Our Readers

Dear Readers:

In order that we might better contribute to your reading enjoyment, we would appreciate your taking a few minutes to respond to the following questions. When completed, please return to the following: Fiction Editor, Barbour Publishing, Inc., P.O. Box 719, Uhrichsville, OH 44683.

1. Did you enjoy reading *A Prairie Christmas*?
   ❏ Very much—I would like to see more books like this.
   ❏ Moderately—I would have enjoyed it more if _____
   _____
   _____

2. What influenced your decision to purchase this book?
   (Check those that apply.)
   ❏ Cover   ❏ Back cover copy   ❏ Title   ❏ Price
   ❏ Friends   ❏ Publicity   ❏ Other

3. Which story was your favorite?
   ❏ *One Wintry Night*   ❏ *The Christmas Necklace*

4. Please check your age range:
   ❏ Under 18   ❏ 18–24   ❏ 25–34
   ❏ 35–45   ❏ 46–55   ❏ Over 55

5. How many hours per week do you read? _____

Name _____

Occupation _____

Address _____

City _____ State _____ Zip _____

E-mail _____

If you enjoyed
A
PRAIRIE
CHRISTMAS
then read:

ALL JINGLED OUT

TWO SWEET AND LIGHT TALES OF "MOM INGENUITY"
IN THE WAKE OF HOLIDAY MAYHEM

All Done with the Dashing by Pamela Dowd
My True Love Gave to Me by Christine Lynxwiler
